4.15

FINDING PETER

FINDING PETER

A TRUE STORY OF THE HAND OF PROVIDENCE AND EVIDENCE OF LIFE AFTER DEATH

William Peter Blatty

REGNERY
PUBLISHING
A Division of Salem Media Group

Regnery® is a registered trademark of Salem Communications Holding Corporation

Library of Congress Cataloging-in-Publication Data

Blatty, William Peter.
  Finding Peter : a true story of the hand of providence and evidence of life after death / William Peter Blatty.
    pages ; cm
  ISBN 978-1-62157-332-6 (hardcover)
  1. Blatty, William Peter. 2. Screenwriters--United States--Biography. 3. Future life. 4. Bereavement. 5. Grief. I. Title.
  PS3552.L392Z46 2015
  813'.54--dc23
  [B]
                    2014049619

Published in the United States by
Regnery Publishing
A Division of Salem Media Group
300 New Jersey Ave NW
Washington, DC 20001
www.Regnery.com

Manufactured in the United States of America

10 9 8 7 6 5 4 3 2 1

Books are available in quantity for promotional or premium use. For information on discounts and terms, please visit our website: www.Regnery.com.

Distributed to the trade by
Perseus Distribution
250 West 57th Street
New York, NY 10107

*For those who have lost a loved one
to that liar and fraud named Death.*

CONTENTS

PART THREE

IS THE UNIVERSE A THOUGHT IN THE MIND OF GOD?

PART FOUR

PROOF OF LIFE

There's a divinity that shapes our ends,
Rough-hew them how we will.

—*Hamlet*, Act V, Scene 2

If, after being asked why the greatest and
most intense of physical pleasures is the
one achieved through the sexual act whose
consummation is essential to the continuation
of human life, and after long and due thought
you continue to believe that evolution lacks
a Purposer, then, friend, I suggest you put
down this book as you are doubtless too
stupid to understand what is in it.

—Anonymous Middle Eastern Sage

A WILD RIDE IN SEARCH OF THE SOUL

When my dear friend Shirley MacLaine and I were chatting over lunch in Malibu last year and I suggested *I Used to Not Believe in All This Shit* as a possible title for her forthcoming book, she smiled warmly, flipped me a delicate "bird" and replied it might serve me very well to do the same. Well, she might have been right except that she was wrong for I'd believed in the supernatural and in a good and giving God ever since at the age of four and in the wilds of the Bronx I had thumb-pudged a penny into a Wrigley's gum machine and not one but *two* packets of gum coughed out.

There. So much for full disclosure. In the meantime, this is me, Bill Blatty, writing in the voice of my comic novels, which is really my own true voice, as it happens, and wanting to share with you the joy of something so extraordinarily wonderful that has blessed me so late in my life, which is the gift of not merely believing but actually knowing there is life after death! All right, let me say it plainly: ever since his passing in 2006, our beloved son Peter has been giving me and his mother almost unremitting evidence of his continuing, active, and unbounded existence and I intend to pass this evidence along to you, for the task of this book, its sole and entire purpose, is to win your belief that human death is a lie and give ease to the hearts of those reading this work who have lost a loved one, most especially a child. But I must go slowly, very slowly, for first I must win your belief in me. Not the writer. The person. Me.

A secondary theme of these headlong jottings straight from the heart is that mysterious something long known to us as "Providence." In grade 3A in a mid-Manhattan public school, Mrs. Gedney, our gray-haired and late-middle-aged spinster teacher, once whirled around suddenly from writing on the blackboard and caught me in the indisputably felonious act of throwing a spitball at the back of the head of a pigtailed, foot-stamping girl named Dulcy who expanded the dimensions of the act of pouting several light-years beyond the ordinary powers of the congenitally sullen. In a fury, her eyes wide and shining with hatred and loathing, Mrs. Gedney shrieked at me in a high, squeaky voice, like some demonically possessed Minnie Mouse, "*You little sneak!*" True. And I mention this because "Providence" to me is the sneaky "spitball" word you can safely use in place of "God" these days without some atheists or the ACLU or "Satanists for Justin Bieber's Right to Exist" wanting to haul you into court or to denounce you as a putz of intergalactic standing afflicted by toenail fungus of the mind, because to them the existence of You-Know-Who helps make the case that we are endowed with souls. So then, fine. So I won't say "God" or even "The Schwartz." Yes, let no one write "obdurate" on my tombstone. As I said, we are strictly talking Providence here, though, for those in good will, kindly notice that I capitalized the "P."

In the meantime, I believe we have a problem of communication, by which I mean that if this non-existent deity were to suddenly appear atop the Chrysler Building at the stroke of noon amid thunder and lightning after darkening the sun and then causing it to slash the incredulous sky with fiery figure eights and Immelmanns by way of showing its "Creator

I.D." before demanding we be kind to one another "or else," for a time most who witnessed this would instantly "believe," though soon enough they would be doubting their senses, citing "mass hallucination" or perhaps "wishful thinking on a stupefying scale," while as for those who retained a grip on their belief, they would be doubted by anyone to whom they recounted it, the exceptions being those who knew the witness so long and so well that lying and self-delusion would be deemed about as likely as the FDA approving the marketing of suicide pills with "a mild laxative side-effect." So what I'm planning to do in the pages that follow is to tell you a very great deal about myself, from my grimy and disheveled boyhood to my supposedly glamorous Hollywood screenwriting days, although only so much of it as I think may be needed to convince you of my truthfulness and credibility when I repeat that, without the slightest doubt, I don't simply believe but rather I *know* there is life after death, and that the multiple firsthand encounters that I'll be giving you as evidence of this aren't coming from some gullible New Age whacko who wasn't born on this planet but in point of fact *landed* here with the manuscript of *The Exorcist* tucked under his arm. And so now may we begin? Yes? Good. Fasten your seat belt.

PART ONE

A Klutz Grows in Brooklyn

ONE

My parents emigrated to the United States from Lebanon on a cattle boat in 1921, and from the moment I toddled into the age of reason my Lebanese mother, a saint in all things in which the heart alone matters, initiated vast attempts at driving me back out of it with incessant verbal blasts about the beauty and wonder of the "old country." "Will-*yam*," she would begin with her inimitable Arabic accent tinged with a delicate touch of French, "Will-*yam*, when you grow up I gonna send you to Lebanon so you can marry an Arab girl. My *God*, Arab girls are beautiful!" Well-meaning neighbors to our Lower East Side apartment made now and then feeble passes at advising my mother not to "nag the boy too much," but trying to intimidate Mama was like buttermilk trying to intimidate Hungarian goulash. A dark-eyed, loving, stubborn, courageous woman, she barreled through life hell-bent on ignoring road signs.

Once, for example, in the summer of 1939, President Franklin D. Roosevelt visited our neighborhood to officiate at the formal opening of the Queens Midtown Tunnel which spilled out onto East 35th Street, just one door down from our apartment building, and, "I wanna meet him," Mama rumbled like Vesuvius when she heard FDR was coming. My uncles—Moses, Elias, and Albert—told her it was "impossible," to which she pityingly responded, "You cuckoo!"

On the day of the ceremony, my mother and I, together with my uncles, were standing at the outer circumference of a cordon of spectators about thirty feet from the president's automobile. In her left hand, Mama held a mysterious, brown paper shopping bag, but I paid no attention to it at the time. All eyes were on FDR as he reached out from his car with a gold-plated scissors and neatly snipped the broad, blue ribbon that stretched from one side of the tunnel entrance to the other. Then, before anyone knew what was happening, my mother was grimly advancing on the president. It must have looked like an assassination attempt because flash-bulbs started exploding, the president dropped the scissors in dread antic-ipation, and a covey of Secret Service men drew their revolvers and surrounded the car.

They were too late. Mama had gotten to the president.

"I wanna shake you hand," she announced, half purr, half growl, and then she reached out and crunched the president's paw in her effortlessly dynamic grip. FDR smiled weakly. Then it happened. Mama leaned over and reached into the mysterious shopping bag and two of the Secret Service men made a dive for her, but they barely got a glove on my mother before she had withdrawn from the bag a large glass jar filled with a murky, rust-colored substance. She handed it to the astonished president.

"Homemake jelly," Mama grunted. "For when you have company."

As I recall it, one of the Secret Service men lunged for the jar, but FDR waved him off and accepted it. "Thank you, Madam," he said.

"*Quince* jelly," my mother added matter-of-factly. "*Lebanese* quince jelly. Delicious!"

The president smiled—it was almost a grin—and shook my mother's hand again. I had to card the man for sheer guts.

Three Secret Service agents escorted Mama back to the spectators' circle, and as her gaze fell upon my uncles her eyes flickered briefly with a glint of victory and satisfaction. She was unstoppable and she knew it.

Mama's irresistible force was once memorialized in a silver loving cup that I'd won in a "Beautiful Baby" contest, and "My *God*, he was beautiful baby!" she would marvel when glancing at the trophy, at times mysteriously capping this performance by turning her head to stare cunningly, if not triumphantly, in my direction while murmuring, "You Mama take good care of you, Will-*yam!*" I never knew what she meant by this until I asked one of my uncles about it, finally, and he reluctantly confided that Mama had "take care" of me during the Zwieback caper by bribing one of the judges, thus rendering me the only living mortal ever to have won a "fixed" beautiful baby contest, my emotions during the course of this revelation being best described, I suppose, as stunningly conflicted, although one of my thoughts back then still piercingly clear was that no Everest was beyond my mother's reach. Her page of life had been printed in boldface.

On the other hand, my father, Peter, was light italics. Many years later, whenever I would mention him in the presence of my Uncle George, "What a quiet man," he would invariably say. A pixieish, introspective sort, Papa separated from my mother when I was three, and I think it was all because of a newspaper. Mama had for years been baffled in her sporadic and impatient attempts to learn written English, and Papa, who'd mastered it quickly, had a little trick of deliberately infuriating her by sinking into an overstuffed chair in the living room, luxuriously rustling and unfolding the evening newspaper, and *reading* it. "Looka him! *Looka* him!" my mother would complain. She was insanely jealous of my father's ability. Of course I'm pretty sure that wasn't all there was to it, but whatever it was, when I was three years old, one evening my Lebanese daddy just folded up his newspaper and silently stole away. I missed him.

Had he hung in there a while longer, my father might have proved a paper-rustling *Coeur de Lion* set against my mother's onrushing Saladin.

But the way things worked out, it was Mama's boat race all the way, and the first language that I conned was Arabic, which is how I was exiled from my peers at four. That's right—*four.* I'm certain about the age because although today I can't remember what I had for breakfast this morning or the name of the pill I take daily to enhance my memory, I have almost total recall of my childhood dating back to my days in a crib, and what I can't remember my mother has filled in, for all my life she has boasted of my feats as a tot. It all began, I think, when I told her I had dreamed of Christ, whereupon she began referring to me as *Il Waheed,* which in Arabic means, "The One," an appellation that soon would give way to a frequent and admittedly not entirely uninteresting variation, which was to cite me as "Will-yam, my Baby Jesus!" for which, as proof, one of Mama's more incredible brags in the presence of strangers or of newly met girls I was trying to impress was, "When he was baby, my Willie he *never dirty his diaper!*" which all in all was a welcome variation, I guess, to her holding out her hand to the girl to shake it while telling her quietly, "You very fat."

At the age of five another "sign" appeared that I was either "The One" or maybe even "J.C." when I made the fatal error of not keeping my mouth shut about another dream that I'd had. Back in those days much entertainment could be found that was innocent, with billboards abounding that advertised movies like *Here Comes the Navy* and *Steamboat Round the Bend* and even certain forms of gambling were viewed with a smile of indulgence, one of which was known as "Playing the Numbers," in which the bettor would pick a three digit number, the winner to be determined by the entry numbers of the horses who won certain pre-designated races at a racetrack in New York, maybe Belmont Park. So one day Mama asked me to "pick a number." I didn't have one. But then some days later, Willie, our apartment building janitor and local "numbers taker," rang the doorbell and asked Mama if she wanted to play. "No, I have no money," Mama answered downheartedly. But then Willie asked if she had any empty milk bottles, which at that time were made of glass and for which you got a penny each in deposit back from the grocer for each bottle you returned.

Mama found five and bet a nickel, and before Willie asked her to pick her number which he would then inscribe on a thumbnail with a pen, I flashed on a strange and vivid dream that I'd had just the night before in which I was looking up at a mysterious man playing a pinball machine. Tall and slender and with an aquiline, slightly hooked nose, he wore a dark blazer jacket and fedora hat with a brightly colored feather tucked into its band as he turned his gaze to me and said simply, "Play 059." That was it. Recollecting it, I blurted out, "Mama, play 059!" Well, she did and for her five-penny bet she won thirty-seven dollars, which would have been great, except that the incident confirmed her in both her belief and her powerful insistence to all within hearing range that I was quite possibly "You-Know-Who."

Some days later, when the boy Sybil of Amsterdam Avenue was prompted to repeat his star-dreamt performance, I forecast the next day's winning number to be 789. It wasn't. Yet I remember standing in the street watching and listening to Mama expressing her first doubts about my hidden divine nature with my Uncle Fred, during which at least once I caught her shifting a sidewise, doubtfully appraising glance in my direction as if wondering if she needed to re-check my diapers, when Fred mildly rebuked her by pointing out that had she played the 789 in "combination"—that day's winner being 978—she would have had a winner.

Nice. But this won me scant acclaim among my snot-nosed peers and made me wishful that I still had a friendship with Frankie, a little girl and playmate of my age at the time, which was five, when we were living for a record-breaking fourteen weeks somewhere far up on Amsterdam Avenue. We would play near the corner of the street making mud pies. Frankie was *muy simpático*, but Mama put an end to that little affair. What happened was that during a routine medical check-up at a public health clinic, an awe-inspiring surfeit of wax had to be removed from my ears and my mother was convinced that I had "caught it" from Frankie. "You catch it from *Frangie!*" she wailed in half anguish, half accusation, and the contradictory and crushing weight of medical opinion in this regard had about as much effect upon her as a weak-jawed, lame-brained mole trying to burrow through Gibraltar on a dare. If Albert Schweitzer had come riding into our kitchen on a unicorn to tell my mother she was wrong, she would merely have roared at him, "You *shurrup*, you crazy! He catch it from *Frangie!*" and the good doctor would have been immensely relieved to get back to Africa and some relatively *gemütlich* and predictable head-hunters. As for Frankie, I was forbidden to speak to her, and as far as that goes, I couldn't bear to look at the hurt in her eyes. Her mouth open, a tiny shovel and pail hanging limply from her hands, "There's mud pies that need makin'," her sorrowful expression seemed to be telling me, and each time I ran across her, I would instinctively poke a finger into my ear, scrape it around a little and wish that I were God. This did not happen.

TWO

ollowing Papa's disappearing act, Mama was left to fend for five of us: my sister Alice, my older brothers Michael, Maurice, and Eddie, and myself. This was actually well below her capabilities. Not that we were among the moneyed Arabs. We were what I'd describe as "comfortably destitute." Mama provided the comfort, but she did it in a way that was maddeningly Lebanese, which was to outfit me in undersized, tattered knickers and then park me at the fountain in front of the Plaza Hotel while she darted in and out among the intermittently halted traffic at the light by the Paris movie theater peddling her "home-make" quince jelly to crusty dowagers and surprised looking wealthy men in homburgs sitting in the back seats of limousines. I was eight and extremely sensitive but whenever I complained about our Park Avenue ploy, my mother would hold high a jar of quince jelly and declaim, "In old country, peddling is honorable profession!" "It isn't just peddling," I would whine, "it's practically begging." But my mother's invariable stopper was to ram a two-penny halvah into my mouth and assure me, "In old country, *begging* is honorable profession!"

Not that "quincing" with Mama was entirely grim, a fact due to her robust sense of humor spouting up from a soul that was a well of good cheer firmly grounded in her faith in a loving God and that one day all things would be right and, much more important, explained. For example, there's that day when we had started out quincing by the Plaza Hotel but then moved to Radio City Music Hall for the Sunday matinee crowds. Something nice happened there: it was March and windy and a gust blew a dollar bill straight at my chest. Years later this would prove to be far more than happenstance or good luck, but rather something profoundly and deeply mysterious which I'll explain when we're farther along. In the meantime, after the Radio City crowds had thinned away, Mama and I moved on, working Park Avenue servants' entries looking for food, especially that deliciously rich freshly home-baked and thickly crusted white bread whose aroma in the chilly March air would at times make me dizzy and faint with longing. Once I saw by a certain slight quivering of Mama's body, as she rang another doorbell, that this time she was going to be pleading to use the bathroom. Nobody answered, and when another ten seconds or so thudded by and I saw Mama's quivering grow at first more pronounced, and then smoothly elide into vigorous shaking, I decided to strike, basing my attack on the time Mama was driving a car that had been taken on a "test drive" from an auto dealership for the day so that all of us kids could take a ride in "the country." Impatient and annoyed by a slowly moving hay truck just ahead of us, Mama had grimly declared, "I gonna pass dat'a truck" with the result that seconds later we were overturned in a ditch. "I gonna pass dat'a truck," I now uttered somberly, and "Willie, you stop!" Mama bade me, giggling. How mightily she dreaded my awesome power, my almost Svengali-like control of her kidneys. "I gonna pass dat'a truck," I repeated remorselessly as Mama rang the bell again repeatedly, frantically, while "Willie, I *kill* you!" she threatened me, weak and convulsed with laughter. Notice the lack of reference to "The One" or to

"Baby Jesus," by the way. It all ended well, for a kindly young housemaid opened the door, sized up the situation with eyes that were wide with wonder and awe and quickly acquiesced to Mama's urgent pleas, thus leaving me alive to strike again some other day.

Meantime, Mama's sense of humor at times had a dark side. I cite, for example, the notorious and still unsolved case of the mysterious two-day disappearance of Tae-Tae, Papa's mother. A tiny and autumn-leaf-frail old woman with cat green eyes beneath a tightly drawn bun of white hair, she rarely ever was seen without a broom in her hands, always broodily muttering while sweeping the floor, which was constantly. When any of us went to the bathroom, for example, when we'd finished she'd come in, use the "johnny mop" on the toilet and then sweep along the path where we'd walked in and out, all the while softly cursing in Arabic. All of this frosted Mama to the eyelids, for she believed that Tae-Tae's sweeping was a deliberate rebuke of Mama's housekeeping, so that when Tae-Tae died at the age of eighty-three, Mama took the news with a deadpan expression as, opening an eye from an afternoon doze, she asked drily, "Did they bury her with her broom?"

Tae-Tae couldn't speak a single word of English, and as a consequence she never dared leave the apartment building unaccompanied since with age her short term memory was almost non-existent and she feared she wouldn't be able to find her way back. But one day Mama declared that "an angel, I forget his name," had told her in a dream that Tae-Tae's problem could be solved by simply putting a chalk-mark, something distinctive, on the front of our building as Tae-Tae's beacon. The plan was implemented and seemed to work well until an unknown assailant placed identical marks on all the other buildings on the street so that when Tae-Tae went out for some air one morning she wasn't found until a day later in a local police station where a patrolman had deposited her after finding her, dazed and weeping, while endlessly wandering up and down along the row of identical markings. She was heard, some said, to cry out the word "*Chara!*" any number of times in an anguished, frustrated voice and, no, I have no idea what it means. The "phantom marker" was never unmasked. Papa was convinced it was an inside job and Maurice, for some reason, was suspected for a while no doubt because of his sly, off-the-wall sense of humor, but I'm pretty well certain the perp was Mama, for whenever the incident was mentioned, she would glance at me sidewise with a grin that was a mixture of slyness and wicked merriment, plus also on one of these occasions she winked.

Not quite so funny, of course, was the time we applied for Home Relief, for when the social worker came calling on us, as we were all three descending in an elevator Mama wound up punching her in the stomach when the woman made the error of asking Mama questions in an obviously patronizing, if not pissily snotty, tone that was compounded by a nasal Bryn Mawr delivery. When the elevator stopped at our floor, Mama chased the proud, educated ditz into the hall, where she ran away whimpering with her questionnaires tightly clutched to her startled bosom. How anyone could feel patronizing or superior in the presence of Mama is something that I never could understand, though I daresay the social worker got the message. As for Mama, she actually couldn't have cared less about Home Relief, for her day's quince-jelly haul was at times substantial. One night I watched her as she sat hunched over the bare, scarred wooden table in our kitchen, which was illuminated only by candlelight since yet again we hadn't paid our electric bill, an event so frequent that I would see more shadows in our apartments than would be found in a hospital disturbed ward for groundhogs. The candlelight cast a moody glow over Mama's handsome and patrician bronzed face, so that she looked like an Arab Ethel Barrymore as she peered up at me craftily and with a sly, merry twinkle in her eyes as she uttered, "Let's hope that your father doesn't come back."

⸺◆⸺

In addition to quincing, Mama employed still another economic dodge. I speak of her ingenious "locked landlord" gambit wherein, in a strategy worthy of Clausewitz, she would pay the first month's rent in advance and then repel all future demands for payment with cries of "You *shurrup*, you crookit landlord! *I know all about you!*" and while the landlord worried over what my mother "knew," we would live rent-free for anywhere from two to four months, depending on how long it took the landlord to either make up his mind or examine his conscience, but don't think I'm complaining inasmuch as it was actually rather broadening, although I never quite got used to the chagrin of skipping home from school to find the silver loving cup I'd "won" in the Beautiful Baby contest leaning crookedly atop a heap of our belongings out on the street. We were famous, in a way, for we were the only nomadic tribe living in New York City. There was some talk of our appearing in Ripley's "Believe It or Not" and had there been a *Guinness Book of Records* in those days we surely would have been in it.

Yet another survival dodge Mama employed—a sort of matter of principle you could say—was never to pay fares for any form of transportation. On subways and busses, she made some adjustment, paying a single fare for herself; she was stout and unable to duck beneath turnstiles or blend into crowds like the Scarlet Pimpernel or a minnow into silvery swarms. Like The Shadow, though, her specialty was clouding men's minds. On the subway, she would push me through the turnstile ahead of her, sneering with a faintly derisive contempt at the impotent bellows from the cashier's cage. If the cashier came after us, Mama would swat him with her purse and cry loudly, "Don' you touch my boy, you lousy!" in a tone that shook with pain and outrage and conveyed the cashier was either a sadist or a pervert, which immediately put him on the defensive. Mama knew instinctively how to crystallize free-floating guilt. She also packed a good wallop with the purse and understood how to crystallize free-floating fear. You might say she was a master of psychology. Adapting to nuances of the problem, she varied her tactics somewhat for busses as, having paid her own fare, she would hustle me quickly toward the back of the bus, although we never got more than a couple of steps before the bus driver shouted, "Hey, hold it! Where's the fare for the kid?" to which Mama always answered, "Warr you mean! He don' pay! He only six year old!" which wasn't always that easy a concept to sell as I was actually tall for a boy of thirteen. I did everything I could to try to make myself shrink, including thinking very hard about the actor Sam Jaffe in full grovel in the title role of the water bearer in the movie *Gunga Din* as he is angrily scolded by Victor McLaglen while adopting any number of self-diminishing postures, so that I still have a quite pronounced slouch to this day. Meantime, as Mama and the driver continued to argue, the other passengers, New Yorkers, always in a hurry, would begin to put considerable heat on the driver to leave us alone and get the show on the road. It was something like a hijacking in reverse where you didn't go to Cuba or anyplace else: my mother and I just held you immobile for a while until finally the ransom was paid: a free ride and no questions for "Baby Jesus."

"I gonna pass dat'a truck."

Yet another fun thing that we did was take trains headed someplace like Albany or Florida. The funnest was when all of my brethren were with me and we hadn't even a single ticket in the group. Mama would stash us all in a restroom as soon as the conductor was seen approaching from the car next to ours, taking tickets. It didn't always work. The conductor would at times try the door, find it locked, and then knock and call, "Tickets!" Inside, we would all hold our breaths and keep silent, although once when the conductor barked, "Okay, I know you're in there!" Alice, forgetting herself, once meekly and quaveringly answered, "Who?"

There would follow the usual harangue from Mama: "Some crook steal da' tickets, you cuckoo lousy!" delivered in the same tone of voice, I would guess, as when God asked Job, "Where were *you* when I was laying the foundations of the world?!" Often the conductor, running a bluff, would tug down on the overhead emergency cord which transmitted a signal to the engineer to stop the train. The conductor would have threatened to put us off, and as the wheels of the train ground slowly to a halt, he would fold his arms, look stern, if not grim, clear his throat, then say "Well?" But then if Mama touched a hand to his arm or even just accidentally brushed him with it while gesturing, he'd look over his shoulder for help and there would shortly be two other conductors, a fireman, a brakeman, and some of the dining car crew in the car with us. But when it came to crowd response, no conductor could in the end outpoint a weeping mother and her wide-eyed little brood. Though at times Mama lost, a preternatural phenomenon requiring a conductor with the heart of a nurse in a convalescent home plus a clear understanding of what it was the conductor was engaged in, which was a personal contest of will, and when the creep was insecure he would actually dump us off the train in the middle of nowhere. Yes. And while I wouldn't want to estimate the number of times this happened, I will say that for a city boy my knowledge of gophers and other rural lore is unexpectedly rich.

My absolute nightmare was for Mama to call out cheerily on a Saturday morning, "Willie, come on, we take da boat to Bear Mountain!"

the boat in question being a sightseeing vessel of the Hudson River Day
Line, while the everpresent, bloodchilling terror was that sooner or later
they would toss us all overboard for failure to produce any tickets. Thus
Mama's sunny Saturday morning announcements always triggered any
number of defensive reactions, such as feigning a cold or, even better, a
coma, though the latter so terrified Mama that I had to abandon it, and
in its place resorted to playing on my past success with "059" by telling
her I had dreamed that the boat had gone down in a sudden storm, and
then adding with a dazed look into space, "No survivors." The first time
I tried this it worked, but then again and again I'd be back to spending
now and then Saturdays on the cruise boat playing hide-and-go-seek with
a ticket collector. At times they would catch us and when this happened
I'd hide in a lifeboat while Mama flew B-52 bombers over reason and
carpet-bombed anything that moved into dust. "Da wind blow da ticket
from my hand!"

Recollecting our experiences on trains, I would spend the whole out-
ing waiting for the captain of the boat to boom out loudly through a
microphone "STOP ENGINE!" and then pass out life preservers to me and
Mama and any of my siblings who were aboard. I then envisioned a chap-
lain giving us a blessing and possibly joining us in a hymn just before they
were to lower us down to the middle of the Hudson River in a dinghy.

"Anything special, son?" he would ask.

"My mother's favorite, Reverend."

"What is it, son?"

"'Fairest Lord Jesus.'"

And lowering our heads we would all clasp hands and bravely sing it.
Eddie and Maurice would be sobbing a little and when we were grabbed
to be put in the dinghy, Alice would say, "Who?" I was a nervous wreck.
Yet I would look and see Mama by the deck rail sunning herself like an
innocent baby seal on a rock in Central Park. Eyes closed, she'd have her
face lifted up to the sun and a gentle salt breeze and she would inhale very
deeply now and then and sigh, "*Chay*," which was also what she did whenever

she slid down into her bath after coming in from quincing on a cold winter's day. It means, "Isn't this terrific!" Meantime, I'd be waiting for burial at sea.

Mama's ability to sail unruffled through even the choppiest of seas was partly a product of her envisioning herself as a dramatic heroine, a dark-skinned Lebanese Joan of Arc under siege by Dauphins and idiot landlords, and she exulted in her role of "A Mother Alone." Her favorite movie (which she had never seen) was *I Remember Mama*, and when she pounced on my big brother Mike one day and demanded, "Who write it?" Mike moodily murmured "Oedipus Rex," which my mother would then always quote as the screenwriter's name, although she pronounced it "Eddie Rizik" which was the name of a Syrian baker on Atlantic Avenue. We didn't see any point in endangering Mike by correcting Mama or, worse, explaining the joke.

Yet behind her brave bluster and a willfully projected aura of total invincibility, I detected, at times—in fact often—a frightened little girl who was forced to wear a threatening mask in order to defend herself from an alien, terrifying world. And, without any question, her heart was huge. Once, for example, she received a solicitation in the mail from Saks Fifth Avenue urging her to open a charge account and shop for goodies there, and so with a shrug of her shoulders and no more than a feeling that she ought to oblige or risk hurting the feelings of whomever had sent her that letter, she opened a charge account—can you believe Saks approved it?—and proceeded to buy sweaters and various other items of clothing which she would promptly give away to anyone she knew who might need them, but then was stunned, if not outraged by the injustice of it all, when Saks sent along a bill with a stream of demands to follow, at first polite and suggesting quick payment, but then growing slightly creepy, then ominous, then openly threatening until finally there came a letter—I'll never forget his name!—from the head of Saks's legal department, a lawyer named George Lincoln, demanding immediate payment or The Gulag. No payment ever was, or could have been made, yet until the end of her life Mama now and then made mention in conversation to "My lawyer, Mr. Lincoln."

Besides playing Robin Hood, in her mind accepting gifts from the rich and giving them over to the needy poor, Mama often did oddly kind things, such as providing free lunches in our kitchen for doddering little old ladies in ratty and ancient fox-fur pieces. "Da poor t'ings," she'd say softly and sadly. One of them, her mind grown feeble, apparently thought that our apartment was a Salvation Army outpost, for she would address my mother as "Major Blatty." Another time, my mother took in an old and once famous opera singer, Madam Jocelyn Horne, who had fallen on evil days. Mama had discovered her out on the sidewalk of our Lexington Avenue apartment in a torrential rain one night, cringing and shivering while leaning against a pile of antique furnishings and possessions which had been freshly carried out to the street following an eviction order for arrears

She's bought a cake from Cushman's.
It's been a good day.

in rent. Upon sizing up her situation, Mama's first impulse was to congratulate the weeping old lady, but she was later horrified to learn that up until this calamity the opera singer had been paying her rent regularly for twenty-two years!

Mama often had me look up the meaning of her dreams in a collection of tattered old dream books that she might have inherited from Madam Horn, her most favored of the collection being the one that once predicted, "You will win one million dollars" before adding the words, "Be patient!" As for my own dreams, the only one I really harbored in those days was that I'd wake up some morning and find myself an Irishman. How I envied the Irish boys their snub noses, pale skins, and incredible reflexes! I had daydreams in which my name was Miles O'Malley or Fairfax McLaughlin, and I had blond hair and was the champion boxer of Ireland, but as it happened I was usually content to look forward to the now-and-then occasions when someone would call me a "dago" or a "wop" for at least the Italians were a majority minority. Meanwhile, I would have given a million dollars for just one crummy little freckle. Piteous pleas of, "Mama, why can't I talk American at home like the other kids?" left her powerfully unmoved, and while my grammar school classmates munched on sandwiches during lunch periods, usually a single thin slice of dry bologna between two slices of Wonder Bread, I was compelled to pick furtively at a dripping brown paper bag heavy with stuffed squash, eggplant compounded with sesame seed, and an occasional morsel of shish kebab, which, let's face it, would have actually been delicious, but, jerk that I was, I was always eager to trade my Lebanese goodies for the dry, meager sandwich, hopelessly hoping, I suppose, that in time I would be able to clog dance and possibly say a few curse words in Gaelic. This too did not happen. Meantime, snub-nosed third-graders would habitually greet my entrance to the lunchroom with raucous cries of, "So your old man's a sheik, huh? So wotta you, a camel?"

Other things began to bug me. Like my name. "Bladdy! Wot kinda Ay-rab name is *Bladdy*?!" was the inevitable, sneering demand of upper form aristocrats like "Garbagehead" Arrigo and "Benny the Spik" whenever they were in search of sport or in a funk of moody brooding over their abysmal grades in deportment. Invariably I would explain that "blatt" was a Lebanese word meaning "tile," which proved to be all my tormentors needed. "Tile, huh? Like wot dey got on battroom floors, huh?" And for weeks afterward, the school rage, when properly executed, was for someone to pop up suddenly in front of me, look deep into my eyes, clap a hand to his forehead, and shout in disbelief: "*Blad*-dy? That ain't a name—that's a *toilet*!"

Yet I had my brief moments. When a frail and perpetually ashen-faced classmate named Timmy Lyons announced to one and all that "I dreamed I saw Christ and he said to me, 'Be a priest,'" I seized on the chance to gain standing by immediately announcing that I'd pretty much had the same dream, except that in mine when Christ said, "Be a priest!" he had also put his hand on my shoulder and *squeezed*, "a sign," I added quietly, "that He very seriously meant it." For a while this had a calming effect on my tormentors as they wondered who I might actually be. But then other problems arose. For one, I'd become acutely self-conscious about my year-round tan, especially since it was pretty well known that I wasn't spending my weekends at the Fontainebleau Hotel in Miami. And then there was Mama and her concept of what the well-dressed Arab youth should wear to school, for she had once seen Freddie Bartholomew in the movie *Little Lord Fauntleroy*, and his wardrobe in that picture became such an *idée fixe* with her that she cut up some velvet drapery material and made up a few suits for me patterned after Fauntleroy's. The colors were all her own idea: they were bright Bedouin reds and purples, and it was grudgingly conceded by several of the older boys at St. Stephen's parochial school that, whatever else, I had "a lotta style." Yes. I did.

After school hours when I wasn't out quincing with Mama, it was less of a strain to sit home and read rather than roam the streets in my wild velvets and invite the usual gibes of the freckle-faced "American" kids in the nabe. The bedroom at the end of one of our apartments had a tiny alcove measuring about three by four feet where I'd fill some of the time every day. I'd placed a beaten-up card table in it with a folding metal chair inside it, pasted two covers of *Action Comics* featuring Superman on the walls, called the place my "Superman Club" and as president would preside over meetings by sitting in the chair for long quiet intervals just staring straight ahead with hands folded and resting in front of me on the table. Now and then I would clear my throat and say, "Well." At the time I was operating, I believe, under the vague but enticing delusion that if I stayed out of the sun I might lose some of my tan, and so I soon became a grammar-school recluse and because I never got out and indulged in sports of any kind, to this day I am incredibly uncoordinated and count myself lucky to be able to catch a grapefruit provided it is tossed to me underhand and slowly and I am given at least a ten second warning before it is thrown. The only thing that kept me from falling on my scimitar back then was the frequent, nomadic changes of address, and the resulting quick turnover in schools and schoolmates who, for a while, would not be derisive. Still, there were problems. I mean, no two schools seemed to maintain identical levels of achievement in their classes, so that while a knowledge of long division won me the rank of genius in some schools, ignorance of fractions disgraced me in others. For years I played a bewildering game of touch-tag between an inferiority complex and megalomania, and more than once I would embarrass myself by giving a recitation in the front of the room and then absent-mindedly returning to a desk and seat I had occupied in the previous school. Sometimes I would attempt to wrest it away from its current occupant, which usually resulted in a fist-fight, and the word got around that "You can't trust them Ay-rabs. They're sneaky in the night." Back in those days kids were constantly solicited to send in box-tops or "the gold seal at the top of your Ovaltine" to become members of the Dick

Tracy, Little Orphan Annie, Lone Ranger clubs, and the like, and they would send you badges and "secret decoder" rings. I was so insecure that I joined these clubs *twice*.

And yet with all the deep stress that should have been caused by never paying fares for any form of travel and the constant evictions for non-payment of rent, I remember wondering what Mama was talking about when I overheard her, speaking of me, tell a lady friend, or maybe it was some social worker at Bellevue Hospital, "How he suffer!" I suspect it was Mama's deep devotion to her Catholic faith and the belief that in the end all would turn out right with the world that was the psychological force field that protected me from pain, although my unconscious mind, it seems, wasn't buying it, since—and putting aside for a moment all those very strange and doubtless false reports of which I still have no memory whatever of my running into health clubs and shouting, "You crummy atheists, you're all gonna freaking die anyway!" at the whirring rows of stationary bikers—the first symptom of what caused Mama to finally take me to Bellevue for intense examination was an uncontrollable physical tic in which for about four or five seconds my upper back and shoulders would contract in an upward, spasmodic jerk, a phenomenon occurring about every ten minutes of my waking day. Significantly, this was happening around the same time my brother Eddie was responding to the stress and the strangeness of our lives in the form of a paralyzing fear of being suffocated in his sleep by swarms of bedbugs, and who, upon my asking how the bedbugs might accomplish this mission, opened his fearfully staring eyes even wider as he pointed an index finger at his nose and said something very quietly about some kind of "clogging" effect. Once he stayed awake staring up at the ceiling for almost two entire nights in a row. Of course, it could have been something other than our edge-of-doom lives that was the cause of this behavior. I'm thinking of the time, at the age of three, when instead of the usual frankincense and myrrh I got a little red pedal-wagon at Christmas from a faraway rich uncle, and Eddie was beside himself because I couldn't get the hang of pushing on the pedals with my feet, an impenetrably mysterious form of locomotion whose invention, had I been even just ten or twelve years older, would have doubtless found me irritably muttering that the pedal-cart's inventors had been Martians just as I do to this day concerning anything to do with electronics. But poor Eddie. He would shuttle up and down the sloping sidewalk outside our apartment building for days, alternating pushing me forward in the pedal-car with stopping to look down at me with a massive incredulity while wondering whether even a three-year-old could be this obdurately, stubbornly dumb, though at times when he did this he would suddenly look away as if worried that this might be a test of his faith in my "Oneness." I don't know. I don't think about it much anymore. As for my "shudderings," while they really didn't bother me, they most certainly bothered Mama. I just wondered how long it would take before she blamed them on Frankie.

By the start of eighth grade I was enrolled at St. Stephen's on East 28th between Third and "Lex," and with graduation and the prospect of high school looming, I had fixed both my heart and my sniveling hopes on Xavier, a Jesuit military school on West 16th. It was fairly close to where we were living that month and I wanted access to the intellectual defense of my Catholic faith for which the Jesuits were renowned and—oh, well, okay: I would also get to wear a dashing military uniform with a gleaming sword sheathed at my side, these the objects of a lust of the mind and heart so strong that at bedtime on the night before I took the school's entrance exam, I knelt my bare knees on an icy February floor and prayed all fifteen decades of the rosary for the intention of winning a scholarship, without which we couldn't possibly afford to pay the tuition, not to mention the uniform, the books, and the wax for polishing the sword. The day before the exam, a St. Stephen's classmate, Mickey Fiorenza, whose father owned a pawn shop, advised that I take no breakfast the morning of the exam but instead drink a glass of orange juice, and when I told him later that I'd struggled through the written exam, he frowned a bit as he asked me, "Was the juice fresh squeezed?" and when I said, "No," he just stared at me

Born to write horror.

coldly, then turned and walked away with a quiet and incredulous gasp of, "My *God!*"

I didn't get the scholarship. But kindly mark the praying of the fifteen decades of the rosary as *Providence: Phase One.*

Don't ask me now. You'll see.

In the meantime, because word had gone out to every landlord in Manhattan, we had to move to Brooklyn where, because of my endless afternoons of isolation and deep reading, I was able to win a scholarship to Brooklyn Prep, a Jesuit school in Crown Heights where I couldn't have felt more out of place than if I'd brought my own bottle to a party at Buckingham Palace, for with the exception of Joe Paterno, who quarterbacked our Prep football team and was also Student Council president, the school was peopled not by mere Irishmen, but by the sons of *wealthy* Irishmen, and it jarred my mother no little, I can tell you, when she noted that none of them wore pants that looked anything like velvet, much less red velvet drapery material. It jarred me too, I guess, mostly because I was wearing the pants. But one thing I liked: you had to eat the "balanced" luncheons in the school cafeteria, and my brown paper lunch bag got the deep six. After a few meals in the cafeteria, though, I was ready to crawl in after the bag. I mean, I discovered that none of the other boys made noise when they chewed their food. I don't mean celery or crackers: I mean *mashed potatoes!* They also didn't lick their fingers or burp mightily, Bedouin style, to signify a satisfactory meal, and after a week or so of school, I always had a private table all to myself. In a way, it was kind of nice, I guess.

One night at dinner I looked over at my mother and said, "Mama, you make noise when you eat," at which she gave me a wild, unexpected look, took my temperature and put me to bed. But the outside world had gotten to me, and I became terribly sensitive about making noise while chewing or, for that matter, swallowing, and for months I refused to drink water in the presence of others for fear of making gulping sounds. I was a nervous wreck. Looking back on it now, I can see that my Arab complex gave me a host of other complexes that were quite unrelated. The chewing, for instance. And for a while there, I was convinced that nobody else in the world had a stomach that rumbled. Only *mine* rumbled. I was different. I was the only boy in my class who saw the movie *The Invisible Man* who didn't afterward wish that he had the ability at times to make himself invisible. With my rumbling, what would be the use? Of course, since that time I've received numerous assurances and testimonials, in crowded elevators mostly, that this was rather murky thinking on my part. At the time though, I thought I was unique.

Well, in fact, there was one thing about me that *was* unique. I didn't mean to get into the paranormal this soon, but it's an absolute fact that no one else in history has ever been singled out for attack by skyborne boiled potatoes. You want paranormal, Bubby, try this. We were living on Pacific Street that month, and whenever my mother sent me to the roof to retrieve or hang out laundry, I was attacked instanter by scores of freshly boiled potatoes that came at me from all directions, and yet from no direction at all. They were just there. So long as we lived at that address, and as often as I went up to the roof, the potatoes came flying at me. As you might well suppose, I've thought about it a number of times since then, and I still can't imagine—on the off-chance that some *human* agency might have been responsible—why any putative attacker would have been waiting by their boiled potato hurler all through the day and week for my rare appearances on the roof. And how come the potatoes were always *freshly boiled*, spattery and steaming, as they whooshed through the Brooklyn air at me? It might have been an Idaho poltergeist at work, but I'm really not sure. Which is not to say that I didn't have a theory while it was happening: I was positive it had something to do with my being Lebanese.

⬩

Mama's nomadic rental tactics continued through my Brooklyn Prep years. The only part of her act that varied was its effect on me: the older and more Americanized I grew, the more humiliating it became. Understand, I'm not griping about the minor inconveniences such as never having my address listed correctly in the school directory, or getting my mail a month late because it had to be forwarded eighteen times. But I *am* still frazzled about the boyhood nightmares in which I imagined myself being evicted from an apartment in full view of a prep school classmate who would then tell all the other kids. I'm even more frazzled about the fact that this nightmare eventually came true.

I was a sophomore at the Prep then, and on the eve of a monster oratorical contest in which I had been entered, I came running home from school and stumbled over my silver loving cup. It was sitting out on the sidewalk in front of our building along with all our other furnishings and possessions, and there was my mother, raising hell with the "crookit landlord." She was feeling pretty perky about it, actually, since we'd squeezed an extra month or two out of that bewildered man of property, and her angry shouting was merely a disguised massive gloat. She also felt morally obligated to give the landlord some measure of satisfaction by pretending to be miserable.

"Will-*yam*, my *Baby Jesus!*" my mother cried out as I approached her, and after an enormous, confidential wink, she fell upon me, sobbing with a wild abandon, and that's when I looked across the street and saw Joe. Joe Paterno. He was taking in the scene with what you might describe as massively restrained incredulity. He knew me from starring as Cyrano de Bergerac in the annual Brooklyn Prep play and had once briefly spoken to me as I was walking out of Otto's, a sandwich and soda shop near the Prep, with the look of having just dipped my hand into an empty bag of candy. About to enter Otto's, Paterno saw the look and stopped me to ask what was wrong, and when I explained to him that the night before I had competed in a citywide oratorical contest in which, except for the judges, almost everyone there thought I had won, Joe put a hand on my shoulder, leaned his face down close to mine and said, "But *you* know you won. What else matters?" Very nice. But I looked away and turned up my coat collar figuring I'd had it because he was bound to "tell all the other kids." He didn't.

That night Mama and I checked into the Pierrepont Hotel in Brooklyn Heights, and at about four-thirty the following morning, "Baby Jesus" was locked in the bathroom desperately memorizing a speech about Thomas Jefferson for an oratorical contest at the Prep to be held that morning. You might say that I was battling several psychological blocks. A compelling orator in her own right, Mama had for years been bombarding my eardrums with a speech that she had learned as a little girl in Lebanon, a speech of welcome—in French—for a bishop visiting her grammar school. She would recite it with great gusto at various but maddeningly frequent moments, such as while waiting for her squash to cook, in the cashier's line at the grocer's, and while waiting at bus stops. The thing about it that grabbed me was that at the time of her *original* delivery my mother had stepped onto a stage, looked at the bishop, and turned to speechless, stupefied jelly, wide-eyed and frozen as a giant popsicle until finally the little Lebanese nuns had to come scurrying out of the wings and carry her off. Now I couldn't get it out of my mind.

At about 6 a.m., Mama opened one eye and rumbled, "I gonna go with you." She did. And at the Prep, when it was finally my turn to speak, I took one look at her standing at the rear of the auditorium, opened my mouth to say "Thomas Jefferson," and instead blurted out five or six words in French and then went utterly and totally blank. A paralyzed half minute of silence followed in which I was incapable of uttering a word, although I think I might have managed a piercing scream, and then, as the assembled student body shifted around noisily in their collapsible metal chairs, my mother took command of the Forum in a manner that would have made Mark Antony's liver melt with envy. "Looka him! *Looka* da poor boy!" she cried out. "My Baby Jesus, he don't sleep all night! How he gonna remember?" One of the judges, a Jesuit who clearly had his own notions concerning the proper application of the name "Baby Jesus," advanced on my mother, and I daresay he never came closer to martyrdom in his lifetime. Mama gripped his cassock up near the collar and lifted him an inch or two off the ground while she delivered a perplexing but passionate lecture on the problems of oratory, and then released him only because she wanted both her arms to be free for gestures while she launched into a spirited delivery—in French—of her famed "greetings to the bishop" speech, which she was using to illustrate the foibles of memory. A mild pandemonium rippled aimlessly through the auditorium: my mother's dynamic French echoed and reverberated, metal chairs made scraping sounds against concrete as students stood up and pushed against one another, straining for a better look at the show while in a corner of the hall, several of the younger and more progressive Jesuits, awake at last to the awesome powers of my mother, were thinking of forming a flying wedge. On stage, a Jesuit who was fluent in French cast anxious, worried looks all around the auditorium, apparently wondering whether a bishop in fact was present. "Nobody ever tells me anything!" he bawled, and what he might have said after that I don't know, because that's when I oozed offstage and out the side door. It was what you might call a day to remember.

For months, I know not how, Mama and I continued to live sans eviction at the Pierrepont in a tiny narrow cubicle with a single bed in which Mama insisted that I sleep, no doubt somehow imagining the room was a stable, while she slept in the only other furnishing, a green and black paisley covered overstuffed chair, and every school night I would take an elevator up to a glassed-in rooftop solarium. Dimly lit and spookily empty almost all of the time, it had little desk areas where amidst the constant thin strains of the Musak I could manage my three-hour homework assignments. It was also my alternate normal world. Outside, on the terrace, in autumn and spring, you could feel the breeze on your skin while you looked out across the East River to the Manhattan skyline, stacked in neat columns of windowed lights. To the right, the Brooklyn Bridge arched gracefully across the dark, still waters below it like a double string of luminescent pearls suspended above black velvet, and now and then, sounding lonely in the darkness, a tugboat would hoot sadly along: it was like the sound of asking, and the river would sit quietly, listening. I was listening, too, mainly for the sound of footsteps, for my ventures to the roof were motivated by the utterly ludicrous yet wistful, persistent hope, that on some magically predestined night a teenaged Irish bobby-soxer would step out on the terrace beside me and say something like, "Isn't the city beautiful at night?" or even better, "You remind me of Cary Grant." This is now the *third* thing that did not happen.

THREE

O n December 8, 1941, the day after Japan attacked Pearl Harbor and when I was in seventh grade at St. Stephen's, my brother Maurice joined the Army Air Corps, and very soon afterward Eddie slipped quietly into the depths of the United States Navy's Submarine Service without even a ripple on the surface of the waters. Sister Alice had just married and hied herself swiftly away to Detroit, and as for my movie star handsome big brother Mike, he had long before run away from home to become an actor while still in his teens and had as yet to make contact with any of the family. Years later we would learn that he had starred on Broadway opposite Mae "Is That Your Gun or Are You Just Real Glad to See Me" West in *Catherine Was Great.* Teaching at the Prep while I was there was a young Jesuit scholastic—meaning not yet a priest—named Tom Bermingham who would one day become head of the New York Province of the Jesuit order as well as the Church's foremost expert on classical Greek, a destiny foreshadowed, in a way, by the fact that, at the request of Joe Paterno, the Jesuit worked almost every day after class or football practice at teaching Joe to read *The Iliad* in the original Greek after Joe heard him say that the words and the cadences were "unbelievably more beautiful" that way. And so anyway, Bermingham decided one day that he would take "Prose and Poetry Bill" and Buddy Brennan, the class "jock," to see the singer Paul Robeson, famous for his rendition of the song "Old Man River," and now starring in a production of Shakespeare's *Othello*. A poignant memory of this event was my discovery many years later that one of the swordsmen flashing across the stage in an early scene was my brother Mike, who was also understudying Jose Ferrer as Iago. Who knew? But what is profoundly risible to recall is that as we were exiting the theater I overheard a woman behind us declaring dejectedly, "I was *so* disappointed Robeson didn't sing!"

Years later, while ambling down a street somewhere in the Broadway theater district, perhaps wistfully checking out theater marquees, without even so much warning as a whispered "Curtain!" Mike suddenly crumpled to the sidewalk, dead. When I asked my sister Alice what had taken him, she just shrugged. She didn't know. But later I came across two things that might well have been the ultimate cause. The first clue was the final penciled notation in a diary I found in Mike's tiny rented attic room on the East Side. It read, "Tired. Broke. Hungry." The second was something else I found among my brother's meager effects, which was a signed studio contract to play the role of Demetrius in a motion picture to be called *The Robe*. The production that Mike was contracted to appear in was canceled, then five years later was revived, but this time with Victor Mature as Demetrius, a role that made him a star. I think Mike died of a broken heart.

In the meantime, with all of my brethren gone and my nose still manifestly unfreckled, at the Prep I sought escape into inner space by plunging into extracurricular activities: writing, acting, debating—all the usual retreat activities for kids with no reflexes and non-Irish parents. In the middle of my sophomore year, largely due to my years of study at Mama's own Actors' Studio on Park Avenue, I was cast in the title role of the Prep's annual dramatic presentation, *Cyrano de Bergerac*, and when I made my entrance on opening night, Mama, who was sitting in the first row of spectators, rumbled, "That's him—that's my Willie!" in a voice that carried out onto Eastern Parkway. But unlike the Thomas Jefferson affair, this time I didn't go to black. I mean, the part was made for me! There was Cyrano with his monstrous nose, and there was the Lebanese Little Lord Fauntleroy with my crushing sense of being an "Arab alone." The play ran three nights, and I would always look forward with excitement, if not vicious glee, to the Act I dueling scene in which I plunged my sword into the character Valvert, who in our production was played by a snub-nosed, freckle-faced Irish kid named Kevin Joyce. Each time, after the "kill," I would smile down upon his inert and potato-battened form and in that exquisite moment it never mattered that my stomach rumbled or that I had ever worn red velvet trousers, for the sword was mightier than the freckle! A middle-aged woman who was sitting beside my mother on opening night remarked—swear to God!—"He'd be such a *handsome* boy! Oh, isn't it a shame about that nose?" and after that I heard a quiet little yip of pain which I took to mean Mama had powerfully jabbed the old ditz with an elbow. On the final night, I was awarded the annual gold medal for excellence in dramatics and floated home on a cloud. I had high hopes, now, that my classmates would quit calling me "Arab." And they did. They started calling me "Nose."

PRACTICE SESSION

Bill Blatty, as Cyrano, is beginning to be irked at the insolence of **ᵃvin Joyce who plays part of De Vallert. Sword play to come!**

Creepy Irish kid (right) about to get it.

FOUR

In the spring of 1946 I graduated from Brooklyn Prep with all the complexes that an eighteen-year-old could possibly accumulate, so much so that I was selected to deliver the traditional Psychotatorian address at commencement. It was a brilliant oration, and everyone agreed afterward that for a teenager it was "remarkably Freudian." Which is probably because up until that point I had been remarkably frustrated. This continued as once again I longed for something that I knew I couldn't have—going away to college. It was out of the question. I doubted we could even afford the books. Then something happened. Mama had invited a lady friend over for an afternoon Thanksgiving luncheon. With the friend came a man—her date I would presume—named Neil Sullivan who taught theology at Georgetown University. That was nearly seventy years ago, yet note, if you will, how clearly and indelibly I remember his name.

Also note that this was *Providence: Phase Two.*

As our guests were leaving and right after Mama had closed our entry door on them, because Sullivan had eaten two and a half helpings of Mama's cooking, she instantly whirled around, commandingly thrusting out her arm to me, forefinger pointing, as she cried out, "*Willie, you gonna go Georgetown!*" I almost laughed. I said, "Mama, what are you talking about? That's a rich kids' school! We couldn't pay the tuition!"

"You *shurrup!*" she explained. "You gonna win scholarship!"

Now not only was Mama deeply religious and a woman of vast and mighty faith, but I had often observed that very often her faith paid off—*or else!* So with no other aim but to appease her and fend off further nudging and nagging, I applied for the scholarship Georgetown awarded once every year to the student who scored highest on the seven-hour College Board entrance exams. I took the subway to Columbia University where I took the tests and ended up convinced that had my father been as rich as Bill Gates, Georgetown wouldn't even accept me, much less give me a scholarship. This isn't hyperbole. It's important you believe it wasn't just my *opinion* I had done so miserably on the test, or some cutesy, if not utterly nauseating, case of phony authorial humility. No, my dears: I absolutely *knew* it!

Upon graduation from the Prep, an ice cream pushcart job I'd lined up fell through, but I was able to get a waiter's job in the Catskills at the Police Recreation Center, a free two-week vacation spa for New York City policemen and their families where again my unconscious found a way of dealing with hidden pain and stress. This time, having found that both my acting ability and my larynx had combined to give me the gift of emitting the ululating, terrifying cry of *The Wolfman* in the movies, on moonless nights I would hide among the brush and trees all around, cutting loose in full howl as quaking residents of the Center were walking back from a spaghetti dinner down the road, a practice of mine that ceased, I must concede, when—once again, swear to God and on my stack of old tattered *Doc Savage* magazines!—I was awakened

from a doze on the outdoor patio of the resort by a rifle-toting policeman who asked me if I knew how to use it, and on my answering "Yes,"
he enlisted me to join a posse of cops in a shoot-on-sight hunt for
me—or as he put it, "That freakin' *thing!*"—during which, though
often tempted to cut loose with just one long, taunting howl, I did
maintain sanity and forbore, and if you think that I'm making this up,
some years later so also in fact did Stuart Rose, then fiction editor of
the *Saturday Evening Post* to whom I'd submitted the story and who
sent it back to me with a warm note advising me that (a) in future I had
to keep the length of my submissions to 3,500 words and (b) that I had
to avoid writing incidents that were "absolutely unbelievable." Yes. True.
But I swear to you, it actually happened exactly as I described. Below is
a picture postcard of the nightly "Trail of Terror" from the little restaurant back to the Police Camp:

DRIVEWAY AT NEW YORK CITY POLICE CAMP, TANNERSVILLE, CATSKILL MTS., N. Y.

Here. It happened here.

In search of someone who might be able to find a home for my story
"Terry and the Werewolf," I sent it to Carl Brandt Sr., then the foremost
literary agent in New York, and here was his reply:

CABLE ADDRESS
BROMASITE. NEW YORK

TELEPHONES
MURRAY HILL 3-5890-1-2-3-4

BRANDT & BRANDT

101 PARK AVENUE

NEW YORK

January 18, 1957

Mr. William Peter Blatty
American Embassy
Beirut, Lebanon

Dear Mr. Blatty:

Your story TERRY AND THE WEREWOLF came in and a couple of us read it. I also spoke to Stuart Rose, who remembered it with pleasure.

I must say that in reading it I had pretty much the same reactions that the Post had. Stories of this sort are just a little bit better if they are a degree or two closer to being believable. If you get the quality of credence into them, you can embroider the incidents into pretty broad farce. I would say that the chances might be slim for this now that the Post has said no in view of our being deprived of the Crowell-Collier market. But there is a chance, and I will show it to a few places and see what I can get in the way of reaction for you.

I think you would do better if you could get the stories a little under twenty pages, as a rule. Also you might make some effort to see what you can do in the field of the short-short story, that is anywhere from three to seven or eight pages.

I think that you should make a go of this if you keep at it.

Sincerely,

Carl Brandt/es

PS: I am returning with this Mr. Rose's letter as you requested.

Oh, well, what can I say? "Same old," comes to mind. In the meantime, speaking of things unbelievable, early in the summer at the Police Camp I received a forwarded letter from Georgetown University telling me I'd won the full scholarship. Really. Yes. The first mad thought that came flashing through my mind was that I must have been the only person who'd applied, while the second was a prayer of thanksgiving for a book I had studied called *Thirty Days to a More Powerful Vocabulary* which led me to use the word "vicarious" in the essay portion of the exam, the employment of words like that by a seventeen-year-old in those days being taken either as a sign of possession or that the Second Coming might well be at hand.

And yet it might have been something else. Remember the fifteen decades of the rosary I said for the intention of winning a scholarship to Xavier? Well, I'm convinced the Blessed Mother had saved the answer to those prayers for when it would matter. For Georgetown. Skeptical? Fine. You'll see. And please be so kind as to mark this current section *Providence: Phase Three.*

FIVE

In orange October I was on my way south along with a battered old G.I. footlocker, a cheap but collegiate-looking cardigan sweater, a briar pipe, a beautifully illustrated edition of *The Confessions of St. Augustine*, and any number of halvah and honey sandwiches, which I munched on greedily all through the four-hour train ride to Georgetown University, where, once on campus, I would snuggle down to Shakespeare and Marlowe, Aquinas and the Hapsburgs, none of whom, it was my clear understanding, were even remotely connected with Lebanon. Was I blue? Are you out of your mind? On my very first day on campus, having been told that the school's colors were blue and gray because at the start of the Civil War half the graduating class joined the Union Army while the other half joined the Confederates, when at sunset I walked out onto my Ryan Dormitory's fourth floor open porch with its view of the mud-brown Potomac River gleaming orange and shattered gold and Northern Virginia on the opposite shore, in my mind I could almost hear, floating thinly across the wide river like a message slipped under the door of time, the ghostly challenge of a Confederate picket and I knew absolutely this wasn't Beirut.

◆

I plunged into dramatics again, in a way, by posing as an Augustinian priest—oh, well, alright, a very *young* Augustinian priest—to kidnap Villanova's mascot, a ferocious wildcat, two weeks before the Georgetown-Villanova football game, the imposture having been necessitated by the fact that the cat was under guard at a secret location because two weeks before, I and two buddies of mine had supposedly kidnapped the Fordham ram. And that's right, I said supposedly, for in fact my fellow Hoyas and I prowled the Fordham campus from about 1 until 4 a.m., following faint and imaginary baaaaing sounds from some haunted meadow of the mind until we realized there *was* no Fordham ram, although nothing daunted and as crooked and brazen as you please, on the way back to Georgetown we stopped by Rutgers University, purchased a full grown ram that *had no horns*, drove it to the front of the *Washington Post* building, got a city desk

1947: Villanova wildcat informing Jerk it would like to speak to the Fordham ram.

editor to come down and eye it and then have it photographed, and the next day, on the front page of the *Post* two major stories were featured: one was about the Soviets exploding an atomic bomb and the other, complete with photo, was about the "kidnapped Fordham ram."

The kidnapping capers warmed me up for real dramatics, tryouts for a part in the Emlyn Williams murder-suspense thriller, *Night Must Fall*, and I got the leading role of Danny, the psychotic, "baby-faced" killer. Thanks to the chutzpah of our director, I got to meet the actor who had starred as Joe Pendleton, my favorite character in my all-time favorite movie, *Here Comes Mr. Jordan*. Robert Montgomery had played Danny in the movie version of *Night Must Fall* and he gave me tips on how to play the part: "Never act menacing. When you walk never swing your arms." This was great. But the *very* best part of playing Danny was that they let me do it with an Irish brogue and believe me, Sean, I was in seventh heaven. It was exhilarating to be someone else.

The polishing and Americanizing process had begun at the Prep, of course, but now that I was away from home I was able to concentrate on

Movie star waits as young putz mulls wisdom of auditioning his werewolf call.

filling in the elements of a new identity, stealing this habit and that grace, this way of dressing and that way of acting, from the hordes of refined, wealthy young gentlemen of fine old New England homes who came to the Georgetown campus to study. I learned that at football games one does not belch to signify approval of a sterling play, and that a gentleman shaves before a "tea dance." I became, in short, a patchwork quilt of the Georgetown student body, and, forgetting that I'd ever worn red velvet trousers, I breathed out a long, happy sigh of relief. But as it turned out, I'd sighed too soon, for like a loving and doting Lebanese Canterville ghost, Mama began haunting the Gothic old battlements of Georgetown, making numerous surprise visits to the campus and overflowing, as usual, with Middle Eastern essences and jars of Lebanese goodies. The better part of me was glad. Once away, I had realized how very much I missed Mama and how larger than life she was. And yet even with the paucity of her now sporadic raids and verbal mortar attacks about Lebanon, the pressure of having to maintain a B+ average for the staggering 31 course hours per week demanded by my Pre-Med/Liberal Arts degree or suffer the loss of my scholarship, combined to give me insomnia. Each night I would roll and toss in my thinly mattressed cot in the Ryan Dorm, and would rarely lose consciousness until long after the bells of the Healy Clock Tower, which was situated close to my room and boomed out the time every quarter hour, had thunderously announced the hour of two. A part of the trouble, I suppose, was the fact that my cot tilted rather alarmingly to the right, and I lived in constant dread of rolling out of it and awakening the corridor prefect who was liable to give me demerits for "uncanny night noises," for at Georgetown the range of offenses punishable by demerits was virtually infinite, and we all lived under a gloomy, nerve-shattering tension.

My sleeplessness at night, combined with having to attend a 5:30 a.m. mass in Dahlgren Chapel every morning, made it nearly impossible for me to remain awake during my early morning classes, so that my fellow collegians took to calling me "The Sleeping Sheik," while my periods of consciousness were referred to as "The Arab Awakening," my perpetual somnolence, in fact, finally leading to a "Can You Top This" incident in which an end-of-class bell found me awakening in a Medieval Latin class with Tom Doyle, a classmate in the row in front of me, staring at me incredulously while declaring, "Blatty, this time you've gone too far!" for with a student lecture scheduled that day and the speaker's topic being "Medieval Musical Instruments," I awakened with my head on the shoulder of the Jesuit teaching the course.

Mama, in the meantime, was getting no sleep at all, for she was lying awake nights dreaming up new ways to Lebanize me. Like the time I was standing with her under the famed "Georgetown Tree," a campus landmark. The Dean of Studies happened along, and I introduced him to my mother. "Well, Mrs. Blatty," smiled the black-robed Jesuit, "and what do you think of Georgetown?" and "Georgetown?!" boomed Mama incredulously. "*George*town?! You ever hear of American University of Beirut? My *God*, is that a university!" I waited for a shower of boiled potatoes to come whistling out of the sky and put us all out of our misery.

I plunged ahead with my college career, growing more and more urbane, more and more embarrassed by reminders of my alien upbringing, so that, by my senior year, I was so polished that my old friends on the East Side would have thrown bottle caps and frozen Milky Ways at me, and in 1950 I graduated with a degree in the liberal arts, Georgetown having dropped the combined A.B.-Pre-Med curriculum, and I having realized that the sight of blood—not mine, just anyone else's—or the thought of cutting into someone's heart or liver or brain and then afterward eating a Double "Big Mac" with fries, began to seem, upon more careful consideration, not exactly "my thing."

I applied for a job with the FBI, and "Mr. *Blatty*," squealed the FBI examiner in disawe, which is a combination of awe and disbelief, "have you actually lived at *all* these addresses?" He was clutching my filled-in questionnaire plus several additional sheets of paper that I'd had to ask for so I could list all the places where I'd lived. "It would take us a *year* to complete a security check!" the examiner rorfled. They turned me down and afterwards so did the CIA. Then I heard there was a writing job open with a local magazine called *Ordnance*, but when the editor asked what I had to offer besides a college diploma, I said, "I speak Arabic pretty fluently," and he threw me out of his office.

Being young and hopelessly hopeful, I then hied myself over to the State Department headquarters in northwest Washington, D.C., where the receptionist greeted my entrance with a brief look of uninterest and then returned to her casual but apparently abortive attempt to clip her fingernails with a stapler. Well, alright, I wasn't wearing my glasses. I said, "Hello. I'd like to join the State Department." There was an annoyed hiatus in her fingernail clipping as she looked up and fixed contemptuous eyes upon my person.

"And what are your qualifications?" she rasped.

"My wit's diseased," I was about to say, but under the sudden, harsh warning of her squinty gaze I sobered up and said gravely, "Well, for one thing, I speak Arabic quite fluently."

Her expression changed into one of great interest. "My Gawd!" she uttered, "How great!" But then suddenly her wide eyes narrowed to apple seeds. "Are you on the Civil Service Register?" she asked portentously.

"What's the Civil Service Register?" I innocently asked, and if you're thinking this wasn't the best thing to say, you're probably right because within moments I found myself alone in the outer corridor. Perplexed, I thought of touching my head to the floor preliminary to seeking refuge in a few simple Yoga exercises when along came a portly gentleman who had a look of some learning about him and so, "What's the Civil Service Register?" I thrust.

"Oh ho ho!" he began a bit strangely, but then proved himself a willing oracle by prophesying unto me that trotting over to Civil Service headquarters and establishing my qualifications would result in having my name pricked down upon a list of eligible-for-hiring civil servants, a list he referred to as "The Register," whereupon I would be eligible to be hired.

Grateful, I thanked him, and raced over to the Civil Service Building. My interview there, in a fan-blown, paper-strewn office, was simple but sublime.

"I want to get on the Register," I said.

Middle-aged and wary, the male interviewer toyed with a paper clip, plunging it now and again into his ear and scraping it around.

"Got any executive experience?" he probed.

I said, "No."

"Ever work for the government before?"

Again, "No."

"Bad," he said.

"Bad?"

He swiveled sideways and stared solemn-faced out a window. "Yeah, bad," he affirmed; "You don't qualify to take our Junior Executive Exam. Only two types of people qualify—people with executive experience and them that's worked for the government before."

"Well, how *do* I get on the Register?" I asked, at which he swiveled back around to me.

"You've got to take a test," he said.

"What kind?"

"Well, there are specialized tests for specialized job slots. Right now and for the next six months we've got only one type of test open and that's for a Rodent Control Specialist."

The notion of becoming the only Arabic-speaking Rodent Control Specialist in the entire U.S. Government Service was seductive in the extreme and I hugged the vision to my bosom like General George S. Patton hugging Marlene Dietrich and whispering in her ear, "I don't *give* a goddamn that you're German!" but after bathing my fevered brow in the fluoridated gushings of a corridor drinking fountain, I decided to think it over again in the pulse-steadying light of dawn, which I did, and eventually decided to lower my horizons by briefly and serially selling Electrolux vacuum cleaners door to door, recklessly driving a careening Gunther Beer truck through the streets of Washington, D.C., and then setting a record for briefness of employment as a reporter for the *Washington Post*. Of the latter two careers, it can be safely affirmed that they did not lack for a certain insouciant, near-hilarious charm.

I'd applied in writing for work as a reporter for the *Post* when, ever wondrously and amazingly, I was summoned to an interview with the paper's now legendary publisher, Henry Wiggins, who after a mere few minutes of Q and A, picked up a telephone and told someone at the other end he was hiring me. "I like him," he said. On a cloud I then met with my prospective immediate superior, and when I asked him what my salary was to be and he answered, "Forty dollars a week," I blanched, murmured something like, "There must be some mistake," then went back up to Henry Wiggins, who, when he saw me entering his office to say, "I can't work for so little pay," out-blanched me by a dozen shades of bloodless white, lowered his eyebrows, made another telephone call, then told me, "You can work in Distribution. That pays more." "How much, sir," I asked, and he answered, "Forty-*five* dollars," at which I did my level best to regain the upper hand in the blanching contest, failed, took the job, showed up for work the next day on a chilly street somewhere in Arlington, Virginia, at four in the morning with an area distribution manager and some tightly grouped runny-nosed delivery boys, their eyes wide and white while glaring up at me balefully like early teenaged pod people. I might have heard a bit of hissing. I'm not sure. All I know is that the next day I quit.

My next employment, six weeks as a Gunther Beer truck driver, provoked an incident of blanching that was as far beyond the Blatty-Wiggins contest as Earth to Andromeda or even Tau Ceti. Need I assure you there were lighthearted moments involved? While making a delivery on Dupont Circle at the height of evening rush hour traffic, for example, I had managed to lock the keys to not only the ignition but also to all the doors inside the truck. No, really. It happened. It's a gift. Moments later I was standing at the sidewalk curb in solidarity with the gridlocked, horn-honking, cursing motorists who couldn't move past my truck on the narrow street and I was angrily shouting for "that goddam idiot truck driver's" blood lest the crowd find me out. Days later, my boss, a sweet-tempered, slightly paunchy middle-aged man in whose cubby-hole office I was sitting glanced up at me numbly from a written report that he had been reading and said tonelessly, "William, all of us here really like you. We like you a lot. But William—what am I supposed to tell Baltimore?" Baltimore was Gunther Beer's HQ, and what he had to tell them was that in a period of a mere six weeks I had burned out the clutches of three different trucks, a record, I've been assured, that still stands.

Not needing any handwriting on the wall to conclude I was "conventionally unemployable," I decided to escape for a time into the military. Can I tell you how refreshing it was that the United States Air Force recruiting sergeant didn't seem to care about where I had lived?I went directly from civilian life into Officer Candidate School at Lackland Air Force Base in San Antonio, Texas, where I immediately acquired something of a reputation as I was the only officer candidate who wore rhinestone scimitars in place of bars on his collar, and as you might well suppose this caused a bit of a stir, but the training officers at Lackland decided to overlook this little symbol of my rebellion and resentment. "He talks Ay-rab," they would say, "and we need him," although precisely what it was that I was needed for by anyone in the known universe hovered in some mist-shrouded cloud of unknowing. Regardless, I graduated, and after our postman-blue hats were tossed high into the air, I was shipped, like Lenin, in a sealed railway car to Washington, D.C., where I became Policy Branch Chief of the U.S. Air Force's Psychological Warfare Division, my most luminous achievement in that post being the formulation of the principle that a five-hundred-pound sack of propaganda leaflets, if dropped from an altitude of sixteen thousand feet and provided that it scored a direct hit, would drive one North Korean soldier approximately four feet into the ground. Which was fine. In fact, *everything* was fine. I mean, at least I was in the *American* Air Force, right? Right?

I am humbled by your show of support.

"What? It's really *six* feet into the ground? Cool!"

PART TWO

How Sneaky Providence Flaunted Its Groove

Late afternoon sunlight followed by plausible rain.

—Beirut *Daily Star* Weather Report, 8/7/1956

SIX

At the end of my four years of military service, I applied for a position with the United States Information Agency, and while awaiting their response I returned to work for United Airlines, although not in Washington, D.C. As a veteran on military leave of absence, I was entitled to pick my station and I chose the midnight to morning reservations shift in Los Angeles so that by day I could dream the impossible and completely self-delusional dream of an acting career in the movies, a pursuit that came terrifyingly close to succeeding.

I had made the rounds of talent agents, none of whom would take me on as a client and all of whom told me that because of my "ethnic looks"—one said I ought to get a nose job—I was a so-called "character" actor who could never get a long-term studio contract as a potential leading man, when, about to give up, in a last-ditch, dying gasp I wrote a letter to Paramount Pictures with a list of my amateur acting credits.

And Paramount *answered*!

Smelling salts! Medic!

On the following day, after several deep breaths in an effort to regain my composure, which already is halfway a lie, I admit it, for in fact I am *never* "composed," I called the number on the message slip, asked for the name of the message sender, and then strove to project an aura of monastic detachment halfway between Father Perrault in *Lost Horizon* and Cher, yet remaining somehow distantly tolerant, perhaps, I suppose, even warm. An audition was arranged, and then another, this one in the studio's "Fish Bowl," a glassed-in, soundproof stage in which the actors, unlike their auditioners, could neither see nor hear those on the other side of the glass. The result, which I present to your dumbfounded, disbelieving gasps, was that William Meiklejohn, the head of Paramount's Talent Division, called me to his office one day to announce that I was to play the third lead in a Robert Taylor western, *The Hangman*. "All we need is for the director to give you a quick once-over, just a formality," Meiklejohn assured me. Minutes later, the director arrived. It was Michael Curtiz, the director of *Casablanca*. Curtiz gave a curt nod to Meiklejohn, sat down on a sofa, looked across the room at me, and then, with his face scrunched up and with a Hungarian accent worthy of the entire staff of the Café Mozart, pronounced firmly, "Ziss is *wrong*! Ziss character is *weak*, very *weak*, and ziss man"—with a gesture he was indicating me—"he has very strong face. He has *leading man* face!" I could have killed him.

"Never mind, kid," Meiklejohn comforted me once Curtiz had left; "We're doing a western with Marlon Brando starring and directing. It's called *One-Eyed Jacks*, and the part of Brando's sidekick, Merced, well, it hasn't been cast yet and I think you'd be perfect for the part. You did say you could ride a horse?" he asked, and "Like the flaming freaking wind," I lied, and "Okay, the part's yours," said the talent chief. "You'll get a call in about six weeks for a costume fitting so don't wander away anywhere, okay?"

In six weeks I got a call, all right, but it was Meiklejohn lamenting that Brando had decided to make his lighting double an actor and had given him the part, but before you start nodding your heads in sympathy while murmuring, "Tush!" and "Tough mangoes!" and the like, let me tell you that one day I would come to understand that the loss of these acting parts was just another case of God—Oh, sorry! I mean *Providence!*—protecting me from things that I want, for had I played a big role in either of those movies and been bitten by "the bug," there is very little question but that "life's mad delusions," when added to my natural tendency to laziness, would have led me to work in some midnight to morning job while awaiting a casting call from my agent on a telephone receiver covered by cobwebs and would never have turned my mind to writing, a vocation that was essential to "The Plan." Therefore mark this as *Providence: Phase Four.*

Blatty the character actor.
"He has *leading man* face!"
Yeah, right.

Fluttering into my mailbox soon after the Paramount Pictures Ride of the Mad March Hare was a letter from the United States Information Agency accepting me into their ranks and so to my tiny apartment in the San Fernando Valley apartment complex called "The Valley Sands" where at times late at night I would spy Bing Crosby on his way to visit his future bride Cathy Lee, and hosted parties where I served Uncle Ben's Instant Mexican Rice and had learned that mixing 7 Up and sauternes wine in a one to two proportion would produce champagne for approximately four and a half minutes, and which I served to struggling would-be actors and co-tenants like Clint Eastwood and Jayne Mansfield and another whose name I've forgotten and was a dead ringer for Rock Hudson who was kept under contract by Hudson's studio just to keep some other studio from hiring him, I bid a fond and affectionate farewell before presenting my hummus stained body and soul at 1776 Pennsylvania Avenue, USIA's Washington headquarters where, bejabbers, the recruitment staff fairly leaped all over me! They girded my breast in plate made of hardened propaganda pamphlets, stuck a Little League pennant in my visor and dubbed me NOVUM CRUSADERUM! There was no niggling talk of Rodent Control tests. Instead, by the end of my fifth week of training, and while there was talk of to what foreign post they would send me, I was summoned to the office of Henry Praeger, a jovial and slightly rotund little man who was then Chief of the Agency's Press Service. My station of service wouldn't be Lebanon, I'd learned with relief, for the Agency's policy was never to send you to the land of your parents' birth lest your thoughts and your judgments wind up "going native."

"Blatty," Praeger jovially began at once, "*guess* where you're going!"

"Ah—Egypt?" I probed.

"No, not Egypt," he replied with the happy smile of one about to bestow an unexpected gift.

"Iraq?"

"No, not Iraq."

"Saudi Arabia? Yemen?"

"Nope."

A sudden cold chill began to shiver through my body.

"Syria? Surely, Syria!" I said weakly, voice quavering.

"No, you lucky stiff! We're sending you to paradise, Blatty! *You're going to Beirut!*"

My whole life passed before me in an instant.

"The—the policy! Wha—what about the policy!" I stammered.

"Don't worry," Praeger answered reassuringly. "We got a waiver. We just lost a guy in Beirut and you're very badly needed there to replace him."

Leaning back, he clasped his hands behind his head. "Excited, Blatty?" I said, "Yes. Yes, I am."

If I'd had a grenade in my hand I would have pulled the pin.

"The Near East Regional Service Center—NERSC for short," Praeger went on, "is our main publishing house servicing the entire Middle East with pamphlets and publications. The guy we just lost there was one of our editors. Got food poisoning eating some goddam weird native jelly."

"Quince?" I asked distantly from some altered state of consciousness.

"What?"

I said, "Nothing. Not important."

"Right. Well, anyway, we can't waste time processing a new replacement. So you're 'it.'"

Yes. I was "it." Against the Agency's ironclad and never before violated policy of never sending personnel to the country of their parents' birth, the Agency was forced to send me to Lebanon. Mark this *Providence: Phase Five.*

SEVEN

In Beirut, I was assigned to be one of the editors of the *News Review*, a propaganda magazine whose widest usage, I would soon come to know, was to be rolled up into cones for the holding of roasted chickpeas sold by grateful pushcart merchants all the way from the Nile to the Euphrates and, other than "a main event to come," in my two years spent at that hapless task, a few things might be worthy of vivid mention, one being Hassan, an Egyptian translator for our Arabic edition who looked and sounded almost exactly like Peter Lorre, in particular during those times when Fran Baker, another editor at NERSC, would present him with an ancient scarab or some other such curio she had spent a fortune to buy while on one of her trips to Cairo, and he would examine it and then tell her with awe and deepest feeling coating his Lorre-like, hissing low tone, "Oh, it's so bee-yoo-tiful, Mrs. Baker! Really! Such loveliness rarely have I seen!" And after Fran had said gushingly, "Thank you, Hassan," he would add in his perfect Peter Lorre impression, "But obviously a fake."

Watching Hassan tell Fran that her scarab is a fake.

During my two-year tour of duty in Beirut, certain incidents in particular illuminate brighter than glue on fire the subject of "MEET YOUR TOTAL PUTZ OF AN AUTHOR." One was travels all over Iraq when Tom Parker, the *News Review*'s editor-in-chief, decided to send me there with an Iraqi photographer named Arshak in search of "cover stories," a quest that would take me from dairy shows in Basra down south to the northern and amazing Kurdish village of Sulaymaniyah where there was actually public lighting in all the streets as well as trade schools for girls and free housing for teachers. But before getting into all of that, equally instructive in the myriad ways in which I am effortlessly able to self-destruct was an incident I think of as "Security

Leak." It has to do with the fact that insidious bacteria were in the air of the country—green-leafed vegetables, for instance, were never to be eaten raw—and no foreigner had ever been known to escape a persistent case of tumultuous tum-tum during his first six months in the country. I was the exception. I was constipated, and how this might relate to my being "The One" cost me many a night of fitful sleep. But I digress.

My condition got serious attention when, after six days without relief, I stopped in at an apothecary on Rue Bliss and asked for a mild laxative.

"*Laxative*?" squealed the incredulous Arab druggist.

"Yes, laxative," I said in a guarded voice, for I had no wish to advertise my condition to the other customers who were quietly padding about fingering compounds and salves.

Eyes wide, his eyebrow still arched upward, the druggist looked me in the eye in silence for a moment, then he mutely drew out a dog-eared book from under the counter and began pawing through the pages of an Arabic-English dictionary. When his ointment-stained finger fell at last on the word he was seeking, he looked up at me in wide-eyed disbelief. "You mean you cannot *go*?" he quavered loudly, and he couldn't have attracted more attention had he shouted, "SHRIMP BOATS IS A-COMIN', THERE'S DANCIN' TONIGHT!" for alert-eared customers were now staring in our direction.

"Yes," I whispered hoarsely, my cheeks flushing red.

"How—how long?" he inquired, coming around to the front of the counter for a closer look at me.

"Six days," I hoarsely whispered.

The druggist's right eyebrow arched up into a hairy sickle, and as he leaned back against the counter for support he inadvertently knocked over a nose-drop display, but he didn't even bother picking up the droppers. People were crowding in closer, and, "C'mon," I said urgently, "have you got any?"

"Got?" the druggist dazedly echoed. "*Got?*" He raised one hand to his forehead. "No. No got. Perhaps—perhaps, *chawaaza*, the main store...." His voice trailed off behind me as I barreled out of there in a panic.

And now there were huddled whisperings and stares whenever I ventured abroad into the marketplace, and as the days dragged on relentlessly, friends and co-workers took to making solicitous inquiries about my condition. At NERSC, the other typesetters adopted the disquieting habit of laying page proofs on my desk and then standing back to regard me silently for a time before shuffling back to their compositors' stalls. And Hassan, the Egyptian translator, I ruefully noticed, was keeping his door slightly ajar so that he could monitor all movements to and from the men's room, no doubt hoping to uncover another "fake."

My sleep during these nights was uneasy and on awaking one morning I realized that things weren't going to get any better when I found beside my breakfast magnesia, pinkly refulgent in the Lebanese morning sun, a letter from Mama, whose contents I wouldn't withhold from you for all the grits in Dixie:

Willie:

Etmekdjian, that dopey Armenian who wrote all my letters, I got rid of him. I told him to write to President Eisenhower for me about the rent, and he said he couldn't because he didn't have the right kind of envelope. Mrs. Quimby, a nice old lady who comes here for free lunch and who has been to school, writes for me now. I told her that when I get the million dollars the dream book said I was going to get, I would let her have some of it.

Willie, last night I dreamed of General de Gaulle. He was in Lebanon when I was a little girl and I think he was in love with me. I dreamed I was with him in a movie house in Damascus and somebody in the film pointed at him and then looked right out at me and shouted, "Watch out, Mary, de Gaulle is no

Frenchman, he's a lousy Irish person!" Willie, what does this mean?

Your loving mother

P.S.: Mr. Blatty, please help me. I'm frightened to death of your mother. She makes me write these letters to Eisenhower and MacArthur and Freddy Bartholomew and Lucky Luciano and Henry Ford and people like that. I don't want to but I'm afraid not to. I'm eighty-three years old and not very strong. Could you speak to your mother?

Begging you!
Stella Quimby

This was also the day I received word that a jar of quince jelly sent to me by Mama—swear to God!—had exploded in the Central Beirut Post Office. I should have known it was a sign that something was coming.

And it did. It was now the eleventh day of my body's refusal to let bygones be bygones, and under the pressure of Social Consciousness, I arose from my desk at about 4:30 and shuffled into the men's room for another try at it. So that my time would not be completely wasted, I took with me some reading material, a third carbon of a classified document marked CONFIDENTIAL. It was a strict Embassy regulation that all classified documents were to be locked in the safe before five o'clock, at which time the Marine Guard would come around checking for violations.

Engrossed in my reading I had completely lost track of the time when suddenly my head jerked up at the sound of authoritative footsteps clacking around the front office. I heard safes and cabinet locks being rattled and tested. It was the Marine Guard! It was five minutes after five!

In my head I heard the voice of the American Ambassador warning me upon my arrival in Lebanon that as an American of Lebanese extraction that "The eyes of Araby are you, *Blatty! You must be above reproach!*" and I made another one of my famed desperation moves: I tore the document into pieces, dropped them all into the toilet, and yanked on the five-foot-long chain. As the thunderous waters came rushing through the pipes, gurgling happily in their hurry to blight the sea, I sighed with relief, and I was about to open the door when I suddenly noticed that the toilet, in a feeble anticlimax to its powerful performance, was in the act of yielding up again one small, torn fragment of the document. I leaned over to peer more closely at it, and slowly the large, black letters C-O-N-F-I-D- began feeding and bubbling upwards!

I stood petrified. The Marine's footsteps had now clacked right up to the door of the men's room, and I heard a knocking and a voice announcing tersely: "Security check!" "Be right out!" I called. And then flushed again. I endured agonizing moments as the waters rushed and tumbled, only to watch horrified as, letter by letter, up again, with maddening slowness, came C-O-N-F-I-D-.

The doorknob rattled and *"I'm coming! I'm coming!"* I shouted wildly, dazed and unbalanced by my circumstances and with one hand I covered up the keyhole, and with the other I flushed again. And again, and again, and again!

On the sixth flush, the incriminating scrap of paper finally gurgled its last farewell, and in a wake of bubbles oozed totally into the great and sullied unknown. Elated, I was about to open the door when I suddenly realized that at last, after eleven days, I had legitimate cause to be in the men's room!

The Marine pounded and shouted furiously all through my triumph, which lasted about a minute and when I finally opened the door, the Marine stood quietly staring at me for several baffled moments. "Bad case, huh?" he said.

"Yeah—real bad," I breathed out heavily, and I felt his curious gaze on my back all the way to the outer door.

As I stepped giddily into the street, I came upon a little Arab boy selling Chiclets, and I half expected him to shout, "Merry Christmas, Mr. Scrooge!"

I was immensely glad when he didn't.

The second promised character study, my journeys up and down Iraq, began in Kirkuk, the biblical city of the Everlasting Fires of Shadrach, Meshach, and Abednego, which in fact were still there, an eternally spouting gas-fed torrent of flame that couldn't even be extinguished by intense Allied aerial bombardment during World War II designed to eliminate them as a beacon for Germany's Luftwaffe. There were also, I discovered, a lot of unemployed one-and-a-half-ton water buffaloes loitering around and always looking to take offense.

Fred Dribble, the USIA Library Officer in Kirkuk, met me and Arshak at the train station with an apology. "We'll have to take a droshky to the library and wait a few hours before you cut up north," he said. "The jeep is being repaired."

"What's wrong with it?" I asked with an unexplained but definitely faintly rising foreboding.

"Clutch trouble," he answered, and I froze, the bombshell word "clutch" awakening a memory of shouted curses and blasting car horns on Dupont Circle, and I was heard to sob quietly all the way to the library where, after a five-hour wait for the jeep to be repaired, Arshak and I were told we could proceed further north.

"Okay, you're all set!" Dribble effused, bursting into the bacterial silence of the library's reading room, and "Shhhhhh!" I replied while holding a finger to my lips as heads all around us popped up like angry Morning Glories. Dribble lowered his voice. "I've put your bags into the jeep. There's also a map in the front seat; I've marked it for you. It's just a fifty-mile drive to Erbil. Sheik Omer Aga, the farmer I think you should interview, lives right at the outskirts—first farm just as you approach the city. I think he's your best bet. He's expecting you, and I'm sure he'll give you a really good story."

"Thanks," I said, as we walked out of the library and into the street. A small crowd had gathered on the sidewalk and they had a strangely expectant air about them. Perhaps it was the intensity of my blanch, since in Iraq a face drained of color is far more noticeable than in Elmira, New York, let us say, although in fact I was dreading something else as the cause.

"What's the attraction?" I asked Dribble, pointing to the crowd.

"Huh? Oh, just curious," he said somewhat evasively. I looked at the jeep. Painted on its side were the large, white letters U.S.I.S. and beside them the Great Seal of the United States. Dribble saw me staring at it. "Show the flag," he said, suddenly smiling brightly; "you know, 'Each One Win One.'" And then he laughed. Weakly.

At this, my premonition of some quiet horror afoot grew deeper and I turned to fix Dribble with a probing stare.

"Is the clutch okay now?" I asked.

He again laughed weakly—*too* weakly—then said, "Sure—I mean, it might stall out on you now and then, but that shouldn't be a problem." Now my stomach began to churn, for not only had I already been informed in passing that Dribble had once seriously considered giving his newborn son the first name "Double," but now in addition to "clutch" he had also just uttered the other word resonant of doom, namely "stall," and I half expected a vulture to drop down with the word on a placard clutched in its beak. I broke off the look and vaulted into the driver's seat while Arshak piled in beside me, camera in hand. "Good luck," said Dribble expressionlessly, staring up at me in a manner that was vaguely disturbing. I turned the key in the ignition, and as the engine started up, the crowd, watching from the sidewalk, burst into applause. I turned an inscrutable look to Dribble. "Fred, why are they applauding?" I asked in a voice that knew the answer. "Sometimes—well, sometimes it doesn't—well, start," Dribble stammered, not daring to return my gaze. He was looking, instead, at the Great Seal of the United States, pondering, no doubt, how all that the Kurds of Kirkuk knew of the power and majesty of the United States was that the only vehicle of its chosen emissary was a jeep that went "sometimes." I looked skyward and saw great-winged buzzards circling the carburetor, and I can tell you, that was quite enough for me and I geared up and accelerated the hell out of there. Brave Kurds swooned and veiled women wept as we drove through the city and out onto the yellow brick road to the dream-like mound city of Erbil, again drawing more ominous applause with our passing.

Our ride was not uneventful, due largely to some bustling foolishness between Arshak and a water buffalo. 'Twas brillig as we tooled through the green-hilled countryside of the north country, and all around us were *tells*, hills that had been formed by the accretion of the rubble of cities or villages that had been built one atop the ruins of the other through the ages. And then in front of us, suddenly, were the twenty or so water buffaloes. As I pressed on the horn they moved ponderously to the side of the road, and everything would have been fine except that Arshak, for no apparent reason, turned impulsively and thumbed his nose at an almost two-ton specimen of the curvy-horned brutes and seconds later I heard the pounding of hoofs behind us, and threw a backward look to see that the buffalo was charging us!

"Arshak, you Iraqi putz!" I roared as I pressed my foot down on the accelerator, but our speed increased only slightly manifesting yet another jeeply eccentricity that Dribble had overlooked in his briefing. I threw another quick glance over my shoulder: "My God, it's gaining on us!" I yelled. I believe it was when I thought of what might happen should the jeep go into one of its frequent stalls that I shouted "*Sha-zam!*" and you can imagine my chagrin when I didn't turn into Captain Marvel. "Arshak, *do* something!" I gritted, and he began throwing flash bulbs into the buffalo's path, but it only served to heighten the beastie's fury, and the photographer, in a gesture of hopeless defiance, again thumbed his nose at it, but this time shouting "Aaaaaagh!" Mysteriously and abruptly the buffalo gave up the chase. May I say that this was good? Yes. I will say it, for barely a minute later the jeep stalled out and Arshak, correctly sensing that this was a memorable moment in my life, took a picture of me as I desperately fumbled with the ignition, and then he looked back to meet the gaze of the silently watching buffalo, but uttered no mocking cry or sound, a phenomenon to which he doubtless owes his life.

Omer Aga, the farmer I was to interview, presented as Conrad Veidt, the villain in *The Thief of Bagdad* complete with black turban and piercing blue eyes that brooked no rebuttal. Although he was a Kurd, he wore no Joseph's coat of many colors and was black-gowned right down to his pointed *samboosiks*, but I certainly wasn't going to make an issue of it. Instead I said, "I bring you greetings from our president!" and while he paused to sort that out, I examined our surroundings. The jeep was parked in front of a rather small adobe dwelling, and behind us, to the west, was a tree-lined stream swarming with geese paddling up and down while quietly grunting profanities in Arabic. On all sides of us were peach and almond orchards, and far in the distance, rising up from the green flatlands like an island floating in the sky, was the mound city of Erbil.

"Tell the sheik," I said to Arshak—for Omer Aga spoke only Kurdish—"that I'd like to stroll around the orchards and ask him a few questions." Arshak sullenly complied, for he was still upset about the buffalo incident, and we began our tour of the farm.

"*Uga buga oola*," said Sheik Aga, or at least something like that, and "These are his almond trees," translated Arshak, inserting a wide-angle lens into his camera.

"Ask him how much his yield has increased since he started getting Point Four advice and assistance." Arshak translated, and "*Pooka marimba casaba*," said the sheik. Arshak looked at me. "He says he gets half as much more now from each acre."

"*Half?*" I marveled loudly, very pleased, but the sheik, apparently thinking I'd expressed disappointment, put his hand to his head as though he had made a mistake, and said, "*Pasta* kostelanetz," and, "He meant *three* times as much," Arshak translated. The sheik, examining an almond blossom, peered sidewise at me slyly. It was clear that he wanted to do his part for Point Four and the *News Review*.

"Well," I said about fifty sheiky exaggerations later, "let's move, Arshak, before that buffalo finds out where we are. You can drive me to Erbil and take the jeep back yourself. I'll take a taxi to Mosul and grab the train back to Baghdad Airport for a plane to Beirut."

Arshak fed this information to the sheik, who said, "*Cascara manon-gaheela koo biki, cha-cha-cha.*"

"He says he is preparing a lunch for you," said Arshak. "Look, there is the cook!"

I looked to where Arshak was pointing to see a bearded old man in white with a thousand Ash Wednesdays all over his robe washing a large cooking utensil in the goose-crap-dappled stream.

My eyes flared wide in dread. "Jesus, tell him we're sorry but we've got to make a train," I said to Arshak. Arshak translated. The sheik spoke again. Arshak paled a little. Then "You cannot refuse," he said quietly. "He has slaughtered a sheep in your honor!" Now *I* turned pale, for I would have to eat the sheep's eye!

I discarded my first mad way of escape, an old ploy of truly desperate and ultimate resort that I'd employed in special cases in the past, which was to assume the fetal position, an action guaranteed to very quickly change the subject from whatever it was to how to get rid of you, but as the means of disposal in the wilds of Iraq might be much more final than I dared to chance, instead I clutched my throat tightly with a hand in a gesture that either bewildered my host, the sheik, or was Kurdish for "I'd rather freaking *die* than not eat this!" although in truth it was just a diversionary tactic so I could reach into the pocket of my raincoat with my other hand for a vial of enterovioform tablets, a potent safeguard against dysentery so long as you swallowed the pills *before* eating. Working at the cap of the pill vial, I swiftly managed to flip it open and shake out two tablets. The problem *now* was how to get them into my mouth without letting Sheik Aga observe the maneuver. I clutched the two tablets and looked the sheik in the eye, and he looked back and smiled—and wouldn't look away. For a while I toyed with the reliable old ploy of pointing to the sky and shouting with the joy of discovery, "Looka the submarine!" but knowing that the innocent sounding English word *kiss* happened to mean the F-bomb in Arabic, I wasn't taking any chances on what "submarine" might mean in Kurdish. I looked at the sheik. The sheik was looking at me. Hard. Meantime, I feigned an elaborate yawn, and courteously holding my hand on my mouth to cover it, I popped in the pills while looking Omer Aga in the eye as I said something—anything—I knew he wouldn't understand, but the old boy wasn't smiling, he was still drilling me with this hard stare and I suddenly feared he knew all! "*Magoolh leilani lipschitz lapaz!*" he scowled darkly at Arshak, and "Very bad, sah!" Arshak translated. "You make yawn, you insult sheik. He make now bad punishment."

"Bad?" I quavered, getting that feeling that you do when you're eight thousand miles from a New York cop and you're not downhill from him. "Yes, bad," repeated Arshak. "Special guest," he went on, "always receive great honor, eye of sheep for eat. Now sheik say you no get eye. Too bad."

"Yeah, too bad," I faintly echoed, and as I nearly fainted from relief, I spilled my *chai* all over the table. The meal was an anti-climax.

Arshak dropped me off at a taxi terminal in Erbil, and he reached for his camera but I said, "No pictures, please!" and kicking the jeep affectionately in the tail pipe, I watched it carry the photographer off into the sunset, a poignant scene marred only when the jeep stalled out a block away. But I could delay no longer. In Mosul, to the east, a train would be waiting for me, but first I wanted to sneak in a quick visit to the excavations at Nineveh, upon whom the "Assyrians had come down like a wolf on the fold." I poured myself into a cab and said, "Nineveh, please, and hurry!"

The cabby drove me to an archaeological excavation site at the outskirts of the city. It was the end of day and we arrived just in time for me to watch as, bathed in the softly glowing roseate light of an enormous orange ball of sun sinking below the rim of the world, an ancient Assyrian white limestone winged lion was being slowly craned up out of the dig. I had never experienced such a sense of mystery. Time itself seemed to hold its breath.

And it was also time to find the Mosul train station.

"Train station," I instructed the driver as I climbed into the taxi's back seat.

The cabbie's brow, always furrowed in a look of vague bewilderment, scrunched up to a higher level as he squinted and said, "*Shew?*"

I said, "Train. Train station. Orient Express."

Staring vacuously, the driver slowly shook his head.

"Train station!" I barked at him. "Choo-choo!" and when he lifted upturned hands with a look of nescience and again shook his head, I embarked upon a ludicrous game of charades in which I hunched myself up on hands and feet atop the back seat in an effort to imitate a locomotive, including churning my legs while making noises such as "Chuffa-chuffa-chuffa!" and at one point emitting an eerie whistle in an effort to simulate the sound of a klaxon. I wasn't able to observe the driver's reaction during this, but suddenly he put the cab into gear and we sailed along merrily, only to stop five minutes later whereupon the driver climbed quickly out of the cab, ran into a building that had two large green lanterns hanging on either side of it, then came hustling out again with two men in uniform. The police!

"Get out, please," one said in English.

I got out.

"What's the problem?" I said.

"What is your name, and where are you from?"

"I'm Bill Blatty, USIS, Beirut. What's wrong?"

The policeman studied me quietly for a moment, then turned and cuffed my toothless young cabby sharply across the cheek while barking at him severely in Arabic. Then he turned back to me: "Nothing is wrong," he said. "A mistake. This miserable camel"—and here he slapped the driver again for emphasis—"said you were a madman. We apologize. Where are you going?"

"To the train station," I said in my sanest voice, always an effort, I'm afraid.

The policeman turned to the cabby and snarling at him in Kurdish, cuffed him twice more. Then he said to me: "The driver will deliver you."

"Deliver me *where*," I snapped weakly, "into the belly of a whale?"

"Why, to the train station," said the policeman.

"I doubt it," I said. The policeman looked at the cabby again. "Yes, I see…I will go with you."

They got me to the Mosul train station, and bundled me onto the Orient Express, bound for Baghdad where I would make plane connections to Beirut. I watched out the window as the policeman waved a smiling good-bye, and then, as the train pulled out, turned to slap the cabby yet again.

Pleasant custom, I thought, as I pondered that dream-painted moment when the winged limestone lion was being lifted up out of the dust of when the world still had morning dew upon it, an image that would haunt me for years to come until at last it would reveal itself, I suspect, to be a link in the improbable chain of events being silently crafted for me by Something Other. And yes. Of course. I mean Providence.

Fred Dribble, Sulaymaniyah's Governor Omer Ali, and the Dauphin attempting an air of competence.

Arshak and the Jerk at the "Everlasting Fires."

In the meantime, "The Main Event" slyly crafted by Providence lay back in Beirut in the form of pretty and petite Bea Russell, the wife of an

American foreign service officer stationed there. She had written an article about her life in Mogadishu when she and her husband were stationed in Somalia, a riveting and bracing account which included, if memory serves, being serially goosed at a U.S. Embassy cocktail party by a recklessly blithe to discretion Somalian Vice Premiere. I was awed to hear the article had been published in the *Saturday Evening Post*, which for aspiring writers was considered the impossible dream. "What … what…what?" I thought. "What's *this*?" I had never seriously contemplated writing as a career. Oh, well, sure: in my time at Brooklyn Prep, a classmate, Frank Caponegro, and I were celebrated in newspapers nationally as "*Tops Among Teens*" for our humorous translations of Cicero's orations in *The Blue Jug*, the Prep's weekly newspaper. But writing? *Real* writing? In my senior year at Georgetown I'd approached a much beloved and one-armed professor, Tibor Kerekes, once tutor to the Hapsburgs and now at Georgetown a teacher of European history, and asked if he thought it wise for me to pursue a course of graduate studies combining scholastic philosophy and English literature, whereupon that good man's brow creased in puzzlement as he looked at me and answered—perhaps because at Georgetown I'd been a tireless contributor of off-the-wall, wildly humorous articles to the campus newspaper, *The Hoya*—"I had always thought you would want to be a writer." Oh, well, maybe once when I was in the fifth grade and I sent a fan letter to *The Shadow* magazine and they published it but spelled my name "Blately," and then again when I entered a *Captain Future* Comics contest for the best twenty-five words "or less" about why *Captain Future* was so great, and I won a dollar prize as the winner but they spelled my last name "Blatig," which between that and "Blately" in *The Shadow* pretty much strangled thoughts of writing as a profession. And yet when I heard about Bea Russell's article, somehow, inexplicably, I found myself thinking, "Hey, come on, if Bea can do it, why can't I? I mean, why shouldn't I try?" Perhaps the thought's genesis was boredom with playing endless rounds of golf on an all-sand course where sometimes a gopher would pop up and steal the ball and you would sometimes use a #2 wood to hit out of a sand trap which actually happened to be the whole course. Whatever the reason, I composed a letter of query intending to send it to several magazines. In fact, I still have an age-yellowed, marked-up copy of the start of that letter (see page 75).

I typed up an original and four copies, placed them in stamped but unaddressed envelopes, and then took them to Paul Khayyat's Book Store across from the American University on Rue Bliss where every morning in the hushed, expectant silence of dawn one could hear a baker singing as he fashioned and baked the morning's bread. In Khayyat's, I scanned the racks in search of five magazines I thought might be interested in my article. I could find only four. The *Saturday Evening Post* wasn't one of them for, to the best of my knowledge at the time, they had never published anything even remotely like what I was proposing for their fires-of-home, toasty warm, and straitlaced pages, but after searching the racks again in vain and unwilling to waste the fifth stamped envelope, I addressed a very badly smudged fifth carbon copy of the query to them. From the four magazines to which I'd sent the clear copies, back came rejection slips with such dizzying speed they must have thought my query letter was in fact a lethal curse from the ancient tomb of some diseased and unpopular Pharaoh. But from the *Satevepost* came *a letter of conditional acceptance!* "Your query," their letter stated, "seems to be a badly smudged carbon copy, and if you are sending this around to other publications we have no interest," which instantly evoked from me a display of moral corruption and lying hypocrisy so breathtaking in its depth and scope as to be unequaled in Middle Eastern history since Saladin earnestly nodded while assuring his captive, Richard the Lion Heart, "Why, yes, I would *love* to hear more about your Jesus!" as I riposted to the *Post* in a tone of lip-quivering outrage and injury: my *God*, how could they *think* of so accusing me!

They ordered up the article, I wrote it and they published it. Go figure.

Letter of Query to Sat Eve Post.
Led to Beirut published article.

THE FOREIGN SERVICE
OF THE
UNITED STATES OF AMERICA

U. S. INFORMATION SERVICE

Sat Ev Post

American Embassy,
Beirut, Lebanon,
~~████~~, 1956.

Dear ~~Esquire~~ Editors,

As editor of "News Review," a weekly USIS publication distributed throughout the Near East area, I find myself continually blotting up impressions of Arabs and Arabisms that are not quite suitable for publication in a U.S. propaganda vehicle. But I thought that perhaps you might be interested in a couple of satirical stories based on my experiences here.

The first article pivots about the fact that, while I look typically American, I speak Arabic quite fluently. Thus, Arabs who are not well acquainted with me discuss all sorts of unusual items—including me—right under my nose, imagining that, naturally, I don't understand a word that they are saying. What this leads to, taken from real-life experiences both here and on a Holy Land pilgrimage, may prove rather amusing.

SAMPLES:

I'm a foreign service officer assigned to one of the Arab States and wherever I go Arabs talk Arabic in front of me and laugh like hell because they know I'm an American and think I can't understand Arabic but they're wrong because I do and the things that they say are very very funny indeed.

Whether it's a goat-skin hassock or camel bells that are involved, the Lebanese merchant will normally not yield up the true selling price of an item without a struggle. It isn't money that's the prize; it is simply a matter of being "one up," and so the merchant's initial asking price is exorbitantly high, leaving just enough slack so that shrewd bargaining will whittle it back down to what he would have settled for in the first place. This never happens when I buy. I make like I won the "pig wrassling" contest in the last Iowa State Fair, and when the merchant I'm dealing with turns to his half-brother and says in mellow Arabic: "Watch me schlom this guy for sixty <u>leera</u> for a twenty <u>leera</u> hassock that I picked up from a one-eyed Kurd out by the ruins at Baalbeck," I simply rivet the hassock with a piercing gaze like Sherlock Holmes and say: "This hassock was obviously made by a one-eyed Kurd somewhere near the ruins at Baalbeck, and I wouldn't give you more than twenty <u>leera</u> for it." I always feel a little sorry for the merchants when I do that, because they almost always give a kind of a sick gasp like a blowfish that's been hauled into a rowboat off Coney Island, and sometimes they lose consciousness altogether and we never get to complete the transaction, but it doesn't happen that way <u>all</u> the time. Do you think it's wrong to do that?

I'm
Invisible
to Arabs

By WILLIAM PETER BLATTY

A U.S. diplomat re-
veals what the people of the
Middle East say about an
American when they think
he can't understand them.

Photographs by Peter Schmid

I heard one of them say, "I think it's Joe Namath."

And so now that I was actually The Dauphin, I thought I was Caesar and, like so many others in that line of work, I overreached, not by, like Nero, burning down Rome and then blaming it on Christians, but by try- ing my hand at fiction, a short story called "Terry and the Werewolf" (see Appendix).

The *Saturday Evening Post*, as I've noted, rejected it as "unbelievable." even though every word in the story about the "werewolf" and my joining a posse to hunt myself actually happened. I mention it here again as a teaching moment: the implausible can be true.

As you will see.

EIGHT

A t the end of my two-year tour of duty in Beirut, I became Director of Publicity at the University of Southern California in Los Angeles, and hoped to become an actor. By night, for almost a year, I posed along the nightclubs of the neon-glittered Sunset Strip as Prince Xairallah el Aswadel Xeer, the "black sheep" son of King Saud of Saudi Arabia. It was research for my next published article in the *Saturday Evening Post* entitled, "They Believed I Was an Arab Prince!"

The gambit was made possible by Frank Hanrahan, a former Georgetown classmate and at the time of my "princing" an FBI agent who would take me around to the famous movie star haunts along the Sunset Strip where he would explain to the owners of nightclubs that he had been saddled by the State Department with the task of being "this pain-in-the-ass Prince's" guide and bodyguard while he "cooled down" from some grave but unspoken problem back home. "It's big," was all Frank would say, but always adding that "His Highness doesn't want any fuss

The Lebanese Dauphin at USC dreaming of the night when he'll get some respect.

made over him, okay?" He also told one and all that the Prince was illiterate not only in English but also in Arabic, so "Try to take it slow with the guy."

Frank, God rest his soul, had carried off this sort of thing before while we were in college. Once in the early morning hours after a prom at the Willard Hotel in D.C., for example, he roamed the halls, at times banging loudly on some hapless guest's door while claiming to be "Detective Vincent Gardena of the vice squad." "Open up!" he'd bark harshly and commandingly. "We know you've got a woman in there!" and on one of these occasions when a male voice meekly answered, "But it's my wife!" Frank's reply was, "Sir, your wife is the complainant!" With prematurely gray hair and a dignified manner abetted by the gray fedora he always wore, even indoors, Frank was a frequenter at the National Press Club claiming to be "Miles O'Malley of the *Toronto Star Messenger.*"

Well known around town as an FBI agent, Frank had total cred, which he would nourish most often when he would drop into a bar at the end of his working day and the bartender at times would lean his head in close to Frank's as he asked him in a guarded tone, "You on a case, Frank?" at which Frank would meet and hold the bartender's gaze with a look at once quietly deadly and yet somehow inscrutable as he lifted his glass to his lips, took a sip, set it down, then looked off and rasped quietly, "Christ, what a world!"

One night early on in the hoax, Frank and I were seated at a lengthy table against the wall at the Mocambo with an elderly woman related to the owner, Miss Mary Morrison, when Frank decided he could safely be expansive when explaining to the woman why the Prince was here. "He's on the lam," Frank confided from the corner of his mouth, his habitual tough guy mode of speaking. I was seated at his right studying a menu while the elderly woman was sitting across from him, and when she pressed Frank asking, "Why?" Frank started to answer, but then noticing me holding the menu upside down, and barely missing a beat, wordlessly turned the menu right side up before turning back to the woman and answering quietly, "He killed someone back in Saudi Arabia." I could hear the woman's sudden intake of breath and in my mind's eye see her jaw dropping open, her eyes widened as she gasped in quiet horror, "You mean he's a *murderer*?" "Yes," Frank answered. "Oh, my God! Who'd he kill?" the woman pressed, and after Frank said, "It was someone he thought was having an affair with one of his wives," her tone totally changed as she pronounced with maternal understanding, "Oh, well, *that's* all right!"

While princing, a favorite gambit had Frank behind the wheel of his car driving who knows where, with me beside him and some nightclub owner or one of his minions sitting in the back, when Frank would irritably complain about the way his car was driving, whereupon the Prince, on cue, would half hiss, half mutter with the delicate trace of an Arabic accent, "What car you like better, Frank?" with the answer always being a wishful, "In my dreams? Oh, well, a Rolls-Royce Corniche, Your Highness," and my reply being, "When iss your birthday, Frank?" thus assuring continued free comps wherever we went while the club's owners and managers salivated as they contemplated what the Prince was going to give them in return. In the meantime, on page 80, the customary offer of proof for your skeptical hearts.

It gets worse. The "Prince" was invited to speak at the Southern California Independent Booksellers' Annual Dinner in Pasadena to promote,

Lower left, his Shameless Highness smirking as he kisses the hand of Mocambo Nightclub owner Mary Morrison. Above left are movie stars Dick Powell, June Allyson, and Regis Toomey, all of whom the Prince induced—by example—into eating their salad course at lunch with their fingers while, above right, in a posed photo by the *Saturday Evening Post* photographer, the Prince with young starlets on the Paramount lot. Below that a photo taken by an NBC Burbank staffer on the occasion of the Prince visiting the filming of *The George Gobel Show*.

with the collusion of the Booksellers' chairman, Lloyd Severe, a non-existent vanity pressbook entitled, "*My Father*"—at the dinner the lout of a Prince pronounced it "my fazzer"—"*King Saud.*" Also on the speaker's dais was that Hungarian epitome of feminine sexiness and glamour, the incomparable Zsa Zsa Gabor touting *Zsa Zsa Gabor: My Story.* Prior to my

"I vant my book back!"

turn at the podium, she had signed her book for me, and after hissing and mumbling idiotically through some indecipherable remarks, I revealed my true identity, prompting Zsa Zsa to turn and look up at me while loudly and sulkily demanding, "I vant my book back!" But I kept it.

While attending Brooklyn Prep, I had worked part-time one summer as an usher at Ebbets Field, the home of "Dem Bums," the Brooklyn Dodgers. They were managed at the time by the colorful and flamboyant Leo "The Lip" Durocher, so nicknamed for harassing umpires by getting within an inch of their faces when excoriating them over an adverse call. Will you now savor with me the very wondrousness of the situation when, Frank Hanrahan having arranged for the Prince to visit the NBC studio in Burbank to watch filming of *The George Gobel Show*, the game of baseball was explained to me by NBC Burbank's head of Public Relations, Leo "The Lip"? Am I sensing a skeptical lift of the eyebrow? Of course. What else is new? Very well then, cast your doubting stare upon *this*:

ONAL BROADCASTING COMPANY, INC.

A SERVICE OF RADIO CORPORATION OF AMERICA

3000 West Alameda Ave., Burbank, California

THORNWALL 5-7000

February 20, 1958

Mr. Bill Blatty
Director of Publicity
University of Southern California
University Park
Los Angeles, 7, California

Dear Prince:

Sorry for taking so long to answer your nice note but I have been out of town for almost a month and things have piled up here in my absence.

Believe me it was my pleasure and it was great meeting and being with you. And if I ever need anything I won't go to the President -- I'll just call you!

Warmest personal regards,

Leo

Leo Durocher

Okay? And then *this*:

Frank, "The Prince," and Leo "The Lip."

After publication of the article, literary agent Carl Brandt Jr., who succeeded his father as head of their agency, sniffily informed me that while
princely impostures were no challenge in La-La Hollywood Land, I would
find myself massively unsuccessful were I to try it in New York. Accepting
the challenge, I asked him to book a reservation at the swankiest, poshest,
and most sophisticated restaurant in New York City, where he was also to
give the instruction to the maitre d', "His Highness wants no fuss." I can't
remember its name, but the restaurant Carl chose was in the upper fifties
between Fifth and Park, and once we were seated several waiters hovered
by our table, one of whom, I recall, while placing a dish of oysters before
me, said "These were flown in fresh from the Gulf especially for you…"
and here he leaned over low, his mouth close to my ear as he finished in a
whisper, "Your Highness." At meal's end, the maitre d' refused a tip for his
service: "No," he said quietly so that no one might overhear, "It was too
great an honor to have you with us, Your Highness." Then he leaned over

to a stack of large manila envelopes and handed one to me. Brow furrowed, I looked to Carl and hissed quietly, "What iss?" whereupon the maitre d' answered, "It's a souvenir menu, Your Highness. For your wife," and when the illiterate, imbecilic disgrace to royalty responded with puzzlement, "But I haff *four* wife," the maitre d' took a beat of motionless silence as he met my gaze, then leaned over and handed me three more of the manila envelopes. I turned to Carl with a look of smug satisfaction. Because of the dark, narrow plastic clip-ons I was wearing, he probably didn't see it.

In the meantime, Providence was leading me into further fandangos and ludicrous farragoes, for the plan had the need for me to start writing novels. Having failed at short-form fiction, such a thought had never entered my mind; never, that is, until, unsolicited, there came to me a letter from one Gray Williams, an editor at McGraw-Hill Publishers. He had been following my humorous magazine articles and asked if I'd ever thought of writing a book. No, I hadn't. Not until then, that is, as in reply I proposed a comic novel in which an American U-2 pilot of Jewish descent who is a former famous football player crash-lands in the fictitious Kingdom of Fawzi Arabia where he is forced to coach a Bedouin football team while the ruler King Fawz blackmails the U.S. government into arranging a bowl game pitting the Fawzian team against Notre Dame as revenge for their cutting the king's son from the Notre Dame squad. Gray Williams loved it but couldn't persuade his boss to put up a $300 advance. Years later I wrote the novel, Doubleday published it; the legendary songwriter Johnny Mercer, whom I'd met at a party at Don Rickles's house, wrote to me offering to do the music and lyrics for a Broadway musical based upon it ("I think we can get this done without spilling too much lemon-rice soup," he observed), while Jerome Robbins, the Broadway director-choreographer of *West Side Story* wanted to direct it, and it finally became a movie starring Shirley MacLaine, Peter Ustinov, and Dick Crenna.

But the musical comedy was not to be, which I'll explain later when a hot fudge sundae has calmed me down. In the meantime I was lost in a dichondra-surrounded tract house in the wilds of the San Fernando Valley,

JOHNNY MERCER
108 VIA KORON
NEWPORT BEACH, CALIFORNIA

1-50

Dear Bill:

    I think the synopsis is by far closer to
being stage material thannthe outline is. I
attach them both.

    It's pretty wild, but it's such an intri-
guing idea with such funny stuff in it, that it
might make it. Of course, you know they say
that satire is what closes in New Haven. However,
I think we could "musicalize" it into the realm
of believability.

    You would require exterior sets of the
campus and practice field. Interior of the
hospital, harem and/or palace, etc. plus
several "walks-acnss" in one.

    You have no spots listed for songs, especi-
ally ballads, and I have a couple of suggestions
about the love interest, comedy characters, and
so on, which might(?) be an improvements or at
least helpful.

    Pardon this typing. I don't try to be
sloppy - it just comes out that way.

    If we took our time about working on this,
and didn't let it interfere with other projects,
we might be able to finish it without too much
blood, sweat and lemon-rice soup. Would you
be willing to call in an experienced musical-
comedy book man? Would you mind if I tried to
do the music as well as the words?

    Good lucj (Arab spelling) on all the other
projects and thanks for sending themto me. I
hope the book is going well. My best to you
and the wife and family.

         (over)   *John*

where the greatest excitement in months was on the occasion of my under-
taking to paint the exterior of my house. Forgetting that an open can of
green paint was perched on a shelf near the top of the ladder, I moved the
ladder, causing the paint to land upside down on my head provoking, when
I'd pulled the damned thing off, an intemperate bellow of "Can painters
freaking *write*??!!!" that carried all the way to a nearby shopping center.

Some of the shoppers were moved to wonder what motion picture comedy was shooting in the neighborhood.

It was around this time, as it happens, that a gray-haired, pin-stripe-suited instrument of Providence sauntered into my USC office in the mortal form of one Bernard Geis. Heading up a brand new "celebrity publishing" venture, he was searching for a writer who for very little pay and even less self-respect would be willing to ghostwrite a book of advice to teenagers. And who was I to ghostwrite for? Grip your chairs with a white-knuckled tightness, my dears. Ready? It was for the very witty and insightfully intelligent (on her own) advice to the lovelorn columnist Abigail van Buren, the original "Dear Abby." Faced with the burden of turning out a column a day filled with sparkling wit and thought, "Abby" had no time for the book. Geis either liked the cut of my jib or didn't want to go on endlessly interviewing writers, and flew me up to San Francisco for an interview with the columnist to the lovelorn—real name Pauline Phillips, or "Popo" to her intimates. I got the job, took an early three-week vacation from USC, had long talks with the columnist, went to work, and on day 21 of my vacation took my product to "Abby" who was herself then vacationing in Palm Springs. She thought the purpose of the meeting was to review my "notes," and was shocked when I gave her a completed manuscript. I mean, how much can you say to kids, especially when there isn't a chance in hell they're going to listen! The book, *Dear Teen-ager*, became a bestseller that won Abby a "Mother of the Year" award for its "matronly wit and wisdom," a champion's garland about which I still am not quite sure how to feel. But the book's success turned out to be that sneaky, spitball-throwing Providence's ploy to move me along on the path of "The Plan," for making an exception to his mandate to publish only books by celebrities, Geis then published my first comic novel, *Which Way to Mecca, Jack?* which gave me a great deal more to think about "than matronly wit and wisdom" when the reviewer for the *San Francisco Chronicle* described me as "*a real live pixie*" and "*a Lebanese leprechaun.*" But never mind. So now here's the way Providence works: After *Mecca Jack*'s publication, I wrote to the producer of the *Tonight Show* (I recall his first name, which was Paul) then hosted by that icon of talk shows, Jack Paar. Asking for a chance to appear on the show, I crafted the letter to be funny and piquant, sent it, forgot it, then was startled and elated to the max when the show's producer *wrote back*! He said I sounded like "a fun person" (You hear that? Not "scary." *Fun!*) and to give him a call whenever next I might happen to be in New York, which of course was the very next day. So what happened next? This: Right after landing at Kennedy Airport I plunked a couple of nickels and dimes into a public phone, called the *Tonight Show* producer and he *invited me to come to the studio! Now!* With my insatiably greedy heart racing, I rushed to the NBC studio where that very afternoon I was interviewed by Jack Paar and almost passed out when he told me that I would *appear on the show that very night!* Awesome! Oh, dream of dreams! But the five minute mark before the end of the show found me despondently standing in the wings with John Carsey, who had interviewed me for the show, watching and listening and biting our lower lips as the segment preceding mine—a singer whose name I can't now remember—went on and on and on until at last, aware that the show was about to be over, I turned to Carsey, shook his hand and thanked him for his trouble. He looked glum and said, "Sorry, kid. Really. Very sorry." I walked away and was almost to the exit door when I froze in my tracks on hearing Paar saying "Peter Blatty!" Startled, I turned around and in seconds I was sitting down with Paar numbly wondering what good I could accomplish in about four and a half minutes. I had underestimated Providence. Frowning as if in puzzlement as he scrutinized me, Paar said, "Listen, your parents are Arabs, right? So where did you get those blue eyes?" and I said, "The Crusades," whereupon the live audience exploded with laughter. And from there it got even better. What mad coincidence, then, could account for the fact that watching me on the show that night in Los Angeles was Eve Ettinger, head of the story department at Columbia Pictures and married to film producer Bill Bloom, who had just had a film treatment roundly rejected by the studio heads. "Bill, come and watch this boy!" she later told me she had called out to him. "He's very funny!" Maybe. But Bill Bloom found me, interviewed me, and hired me to rewrite the rejected treatment. It went to screenplay, then was made into the movie *The Man from the Diners' Club* starring the wonderful (*The Secret Life of Walter Mitty*) Danny Kaye. It also launched my movie-writing career, another vital element of "The Plan."

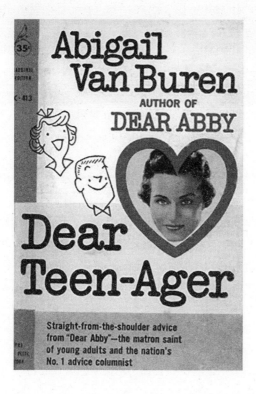

Tucked away on a shelf among some liquor bottles in the bar of my home rests an Oscar statuette. Because I no longer live in Tinseltown but in a place that my friend and former roommate, Warren Beatty—Yes! We were roommates for about six months! Absorb it!—once described to me as "Hollywood with homely people," namely Washington, D.C., whenever new friends come to dinner and happen to get a glimpse of that glittering, serpent-tongued idol, I would ask them to pick it up. Then "Godawful heavy," I would say, "don't you think?" Yes. It is. And that's because it's a metaphor for Hollywood: the outer coating is solid gold but the statuette's interior is made of lead. Hollywood is glamorous? Well, whenever you think so, contemplate this: In the 1955 motion picture *Kismet*, the director, Vincente Minnelli, wanted a close-up of a peacock unfurling the multi-colored splendor of its wings in a wide-angle shot of the scene at the high point of the song *A Stranger in Paradise*, and when the bird would not cooperate, Minnelli ordered the bird to be poked with a pole that had a sharply pointed metal tip at its end. Watch the film and as the song approaches its climactic high point, you will notice how the peacock is nervously rearing back in spasmodic little backward jerks. It knew what was coming.

Must we talk about my movie career? Well, I suppose we must, if only for the sake of getting to a point where I can ask you directly which you would find easier to believe: that at a dinner party at comedian Richard Pryor's home, I saw a five by six oil painting levitate; that while cruising along Sunset Boulevard with Bela Lugosi, the terrifying Drac-ula of filmdom in the passenger seat beside me, he suddenly cried out in alarm and with that inimitable Transylvanian accent, "Lewk *OUT* for de *DOG!*"; or that the author of *The Exorcist* also penned the first draft screenplay of *Viva Las Vegas* starring Elvis Presley?

You're thinking it over? Good. And while you're at it, think about *this*: that long before *The Exorcist*, not only was I a now and then guest on *The Tonight Show* with Johnny Carson but in his opening mono-logue on one of those nights, after taking a swing with an imaginary golf club, Johnny announced, "Bill Blatty's backstage. Bill's a wild man," *not* "He has fangs and tells scary stories," for I was known then for making people laugh, for comedic books and films, although two of my funniest bits on Johnny's show, I must confess, were framed in a certain tragedy and darkness, first, and then later in hyper-improbability. You see, on January 17, 1966, I was a guest on the show to promote my comic novel *Twinkle, Twinkle, "Killer" Kane!* which centered on an astronaut who the day before a scheduled space shot refuses to go to the Moon on the grounds, as he puts it, that it would be "naughty, vulgar, uncouth and in any case bad for my skin," while by sheerest coincidence another guest on the show was Charlie Manna, the stand-up comedian who at the time was quite famous for his stand-up monologue about an astronaut who refuses to go to the Moon without his coloring book and crayons. In my guest turn I elected to read for the audience a brief excerpt from the novel in which, at a secret center set up by the military to study apparent psychosis in a growing number of military officers during the Vietnam War, the base commanding officer, a psychiatrist, reads aloud from the astronaut's case file: "Two days prior to a scheduled space shot, subject officer, while dining on the base, was observed to pick up a plastic catsup bottle, squeeze a thin red line across his throat, and then to stagger and fall heavily across a table then occupied by the director of the National Aeronautics and Space Administration, gurgling, 'Don't—order—the swordfish.'" Johnny laughed so hard he tilted back in his chair and fell over backwards to the floor. After the show, my agent, Carl Brandt the younger, and I found a bar with a television where we planned to watch my impending "hotness" only to discover that the Johnny show had been preempted by coverage of the *Apollo 1* tragedy in which three American astronauts died after fire swept through the *Apollo* spacecraft designed for a manned flight to the Moon during rehearsals at Cape Kennedy.

Eleven years later in an appearance on Johnny's show to plug a reissue of the astronaut novel, I again read aloud the swordfish bit and here you will find me extremely understanding should you start to hear the theme music from the TV series *The Twilight Zone* because once again Johnny laughed so hard he *fell over backward in his chair*! How unbelievable is *that*? Well, it's true. It's a fact. It's on film.

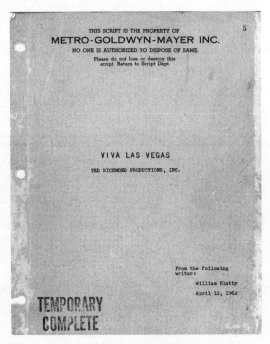

"The truth is out there!"

And so what does all of this have to do with my promise of firsthand evidence of life after death? Everything. When someone tells you it isn't just a song but that stars are *really* falling on Alabama, it behooves you to know the character and credibility of the source, which I'm working on, okay? Patience.

NINE

In my first week of work on *The Man from the Diners' Club,* producer Bill Bloom quickly taught me the technical elements of the screenplay format, and as the writing progressed he would often make memorable pronouncements about the movie business such as, "If the ancient Greeks had neon, they would have used it," or "In the age of Pericles there was also Sam Briskin," the latter then being head of Columbia Pictures and whose name again came up when I asked Bloom why he wanted me to have the stripper in the film not say, "Okay there, Daddy," and Bloom answered, "Because Sam Briskin will look up from the script and say, "What the hell's this? The guy's not her father!" Another of Bloom's professional advisories was that I should avoid what he described as "The Hungarian First Act," this being the laying out of a spellbinding opening for which no third act resolution could possibly be found, recounting for me as an example S. J. Perelman's description of a story problem presented to him by a panel of Hollywood studio executives. "It's a foggy night on a

London street," he is told, this followed by a distant, evenly spaced sound that eventually turns out to be emanating from a slowly approaching peg-legged man in a dark coat and a hat that hides his face. He stops, draws a skein of keys from a coat pocket, unlocks a door, enters, slowly descends a steep circular stairway, the peg leg continuing its ominous, steady *thump* (pause) *thump*, until at last the man unlocks a massive iron door disclosing a stone chamber in which a dozen or so beautiful, nearly naked women are chained to a wall, and when the peg-legged man withdraws a large hypodermic from a pocket of his coat and begins to approach them, the women scream in terror. "Now then, here's our problem," the studio president tells Perelman, "the plot point we're stuck on that we need you to solve. What kind of business is this guy in?" Bloom then went on to assert that the United States had triggered the Hungarian revolution by sending sky-writing planes over Budapest delivering the message, "WE HAVE THIRD ACTS!" And in that first week when I'd told him that Kim Novak had smiled at me as we passed one another in the entry lobby, he delivered the most memorable statement of all, which was the gravely delivered warning that "The first principle of nature is 'Never talk to actors.'" About three weeks later I found out why.

My office was on the third floor of Columbia Pictures on Gower Street just off Sunset Boulevard. After handing pages to my secretary to type in a finished form, I would sometimes light a cigarette and lean my shoulder against the jamb of the open door looking out to a corridor studded with doors that bore the nameplates of Hollywood luminaries far beyond my talent and station, and it was on one of these occasions that, as I looked to my right, from around a corner and striding toward me steadily there appeared—gasp! holy wizongahila!—"Sgt. Warden" in the classic film *From Here to Eternity*, superstar Burt Lancaster! Wearing a baseball cap, jeans, and tennies, his icy blue eyes were fixed on mine as closer and closer he came until, "Good morning," I said to him warmly, whereupon he turned his gaze straight ahead and walked by without a word. Within days the scenario almost repeated itself, except that this time as Lancaster approached me with that same arctic stare, I scowled and turned around to go back into my office just as I heard him say, "Hello there!" Miffed and repentant, a week later I had a chance to redeem myself. So what happened? Lancaster walked toward me, eyes again locked on mine, I said, "Good morning," and he walked on past me with as frosty a silence as the Hubbard Glacier. I could hear the gentle crickling sound of ice shards breaking off and then plopping down softly into quiet waters. But then sometime following this snub, at the end of the working day when I found myself waiting for an elevator while holding a box containing a cheesecake I had purchased over the lunch hour, I sensed a tall presence looming beside me. I glanced up and to the side and then quickly away. It was "Sgt. Warden"! The star's icy gaze was on the elevator door. Within moments it opened, we both entered the elevator and I was staring straight ahead when I almost flinched, startled by a voice. Lancaster's! My God! He was *talking* to me! "What've you got in the box?" I heard him chummily ask. Frozen in my shoes, my eyes popping a little as I continued staring straight ahead I answered dazedly, "Cheesecake." "Oh, really? What kind?" "Caramel Peach Bonanza." "Where'd you get it?" I said, "Per-Al's," which is the last of the exchange that I remember, except that Lancaster followed me out to Gower Street and crossed over to the parking lot with me while unremittingly and ceaselessly chatting me up all the way to my car, then even motioning me to roll my car window down, after which he leaned over, still talking and resting crossed arms on the window jamb until he heard the sound of my VW bug's ignition throbbing to life, at which point he straightened up and waved a hand as if in good-bye. As I pulled away I heard him shouting something after me, but I couldn't make it out. It might have been something about the cheesecake.

A week or so later I was standing in my office door for a cigarette break when around the corner he came, Elmer Gantry, Sgt. Warden, and eventual Academy Award winner for *Atlantic City*, his face an expressionless mask and his gaze, as usual, locked on mine. I smiled and with the hand that was holding the cigarette, I waved a little hello. He turned away his head and walked past me without a word.

* * *

Besides his early caution against talking to actors, once Columbia had given the green light to the *Diners' Club* film, Bloom gave me yet another warning. "By the time this picture gets released," he said somberly, "you'll have had a minimum of fifty heartaches." He also said, "You really never know what's going to happen," as evidence for which he told me he'd once produced a film written by "Ace" Goodman, the funniest screenwriter of comedy of his day, citing as an example of Goodman's wit a scene in which George Gobel is sitting in a lounge chair on the deck of a cruise ship next to someone who remarks that a certain character in the film "has a plate in his head" whereupon Gobel points to the ship's social director as she approaches, saying, "See this woman? She has service for eight." And yet studded with such dialogue, Bloom cautioned, the film was a box office flop. And so it was with some anxiety that I attended the sneak preview of *The Man from the Diners' Club* at a theater on Ventura Boulevard in the San Fernando Valley, but then, "Oh, good," as my case of nerves soon was banished when the audience unremittingly laughed, or more often guffawed, at every gag, at times drowning out dialogue for many seconds, and at the end of the screening a broadly grinning, if not rapturous, Bill Bloom gave me a congratulatory hug. The film was released and was a box office dud.

In the future I would learn a way of dealing with the feelings of aggression that the promised heartbreaks sometimes triggered, and it was from Arthur Jacobs, the producer of the *Planet of the Apes* hit films. At the time we were both working on a project at Fox, he on the ape saga and I on *John Goldfarb, Please Come Home!* My office being very close to his, and his door always open, one day I simply sauntered into his office, introduced myself, and within moments Jacobs, a former movie publicist, took pride and pleasure in showing me sketches of ape masks designed for his film. And then I saw it. It was on his desk, a very large model of a commercial airliner. Through its little windows I could see tiny model passengers here and there and when I said, "What's that?" Jacobs answered, "It's 'The Plane.' I have enemies," he explained, "and I put them aboard" and then went on to explain that while "The Plane" flew forever without ever touching down, each passenger was seated beside his worst enemy, every meal was reheated chicken croquettes, and the inflight movie for all of eternity was an endless repetition at each seat of the worst commercial movie disaster in that passenger's career. "Anyone you'd like to put aboard?" Jacobs asked me with a lilt in his tone. I gave him a name and he curtly said, "Wait List," which brings me to the moral of this story, which is that for some time afterward I tried as best I could to merely "Wait List" the people whom I blamed for my heartbreaks rather than confirming them onto the "The Plane." Yes, for quite some time. I'm talking *weeks*.

Back from the future, meantime, they'd strongly anticipated that the *Diners' Club* film would be a hit, so Columbia had commissioned me to develop another comedy screenplay for Bloom, and while working on stage one of the process, an extended outline known as "the treatment," there were so many times when, with freshly typed pages in hand for his approval, I'd find the producer seated at his desk, hunched over and with his head slightly bent and tilted to the side and his face reflecting melancholy wistfulness as he listened to a taped recording he had made of the audience's laughter at the sneak preview screening of *The Man from the Diners' Club*. Sometimes he didn't seem to see or hear me and I'd lay the pages on his desk and then close the door quietly behind me so you couldn't even hear the little click of the lock.

Many months later Danny Kaye dispatched me to London to do some script doctoring on *Five Pieces of Maria*, a comedy he was to star in with Melina Mercouri, the Greek actress who had just starred in the smash hit *Never on Sunday* directed by her husband Jules Dassin. The script, by the writing team of Panama and Frank who had written most of the Bing

Crosby–Bob Hope "Road" movies, was in so much trouble that once, when I dropped by Dassin's office, Melina, who'd been chatting with the receptionist, looked up at me with haunted eyes and an expression as depressed as that of the mother of the Maccabees on hearing a male voice calling out, "Next!" She wanted so desperately to be out of this picture. And fall apart, at last, it did, although something very nice was to come out of it.

A few years later, in a role reversal of the time Father Bermingham took me to see Paul Robeson in *Othello*, I took him to Broadway to see Stephen Sondheim's *A Little Night Music*. At the break when we went outside for a smoke I spotted Julie Dassin and Melina Mercouri in the crowd. I left Father Tom, went over to the Dassins and after hellos and much surprise I asked if they would mind if I brought the Jesuit over to meet them. They both murmured assent, though I saw Melina look slightly pained while Dassin rolled his eyes as he looked up and away. Father Tom, the famed ancient Greek scholar was now head of the New York Province of the Jesuit order. When I came back with him to the Dassins, Melina offered him the "cold fish" handshake, but then her eyes grew wide, first with wonder and then radiant delight as my Jesuit teacher of old rattled off a long string of fluent Greek! It made me feel useful for a change.

Speaking of which, Danny Kaye surely had the most giving heart of any movie star I ever met. Once, for instance, he invited me to his house for a bite to eat before driving to the Greek Theater for his one-man show's opening night. What he didn't tell me was that Cary Grant and playwright Clifford Odets were also invited. I arrived at his house wearing chinos and a cardigan sweater. After introducing me to Odets, who was wearing suit and tie, Danny went to a sideboard, picked up a phone, dialed Grant's number, and when the star's haughtily British accented butler picked up, I heard: "It's Mr. Kaye, Soames, let me speak to Mr. Grant." Silence as Kaye listened. Then, "What is he wearing?" I heard. And again Kaye listened, but then turned his back on us so that I couldn't hear him clearly anymore. About ten minutes later, the doorbell rang. It was Grant. He was wearing a sweater. "Soames told me you were wearing a jacket and tie," Danny said.

Grant answered, "Well, I was but then Soames came running out to me and said, "Mr. Grant, sir, Mr. Kaye just phoned and he said you were to take off the fucking jacket and put on a sweater!"

When Grant was introduced to me and sat down at the table, all I could think of to say, my eyes big as saucers, was "I've seen *Gunga Din* twenty times!" to which the superstar responded, "Whadja wanna do a thing like that for?" in just the same way he'd said the same words in *Gunga Din*. Frozen inside a block of awe, I couldn't eat and sat numb and stiff all through the dinner and might actually have left my body at some point because I can't remember another word of the conversation either at the table or the drive to and back from the theater except for when Danny asked us to name our favorite snack after sex, and Odets, after thoughtful consideration, said, "A little chopped liver on a piece of rye with a glass of beer." I can't remember Grant's answer, and for all I know my answer could have been "Twinkies."

Another fun instance of Kaye's giving heart was when, after I'd told him a few stories about Mama, he decided he just had to meet her. She was living in San Diego then with my brother Eddie and Eddie's wife, Eve, and one day Danny flew me there in his Piper Cub. I called Eddie beforehand to let him know we were coming. "Danny Kaye? Danny *Kaye*?" Eddie exclaimed incredulously, his voice quavering. I could tell he was squeezing his phone in a death grip for my own receiver had just turned from beige to dead white and from the moment we arrived, Eddie was totally unglued. Mama, however, sitting at a table set for lunch across from Danny, seemed completely unmoved. Her manner was regal, warmly charmed and at the same time slightly bemused as she asked him, "You Joosh?"

"Yes, I'm Jewish."

"Some da Joosh nice people," Mama told him benignly.

Danny laughed while from the kitchen you could hear the sound of Eddie dropping a bowl of stuffed squash to the floor.

Besides the joy of his company, Danny gave me many other gifts. One was the time he asked me if I had any secret weaknesses. "My father once said to me," he then confided, "that when God gives great gifts, he always takes a little something away," a comment that triggered some helpful self-reflection on my part. Another gift was Danny's recounting of an audience with pudgy, little, merry-faced Pope John XXIII. Standing in a reception line in the Vatican was the great comedian Jimmy Durante, he of the Cyrano-emulating nose, and when the pope moved from him to Danny, Kaye noticed he seemed distracted, with his glance frequently shifting over to Durante and then back until, finally, unable to resist the powerful impulse consuming him, the pope stepped back in front of Durante and with that special smile of satisfaction that comes with requital of intense desire, he rubbed a finger up and down the comedian's nose!

In the meantime, my Hollywood career advanced. Once back from London and *Five Pieces of Maria*, I somehow found myself in a dressing room trailer on the Paramount lot trying to sell an idea for a movie to Shirley MacLaine and her manager, Alan Lee, that had occurred to me in the shower after hearing a news report of U-2 pilot Francis Gary Powers crash-landing in the Soviet Union. My twist on the event was that an American U-2 pilot, once nicknamed "Wrong Way" after running 97 yards into his own team's end zone in a college football game, goes off course en route to the Soviet Union, crash lands in the mythical kingdom of Fawzi Arabia, and is forced by an Arabian potentate to coach a Bedouin football team that wants to play Notre Dame. I won't go on any further about it as the plot gets a little bit crazy after that, except to say that Shirley was to star as an investigative reporter. Shirley loved it, although among my regrets about the picture, along with Peter Lorre's death while en route to a costume fitting for the role of the king's factotum, Mahmoud, was that she nixed the notion of taking it to Broadway, Jerome Robbins and Johnny Mercer notwithstanding. She wanted it to go straight to the screen. Fine. Her call. So I wrote the screenplay, J. Lee Thompson, the director of *The Guns of Navarone*, agreed to direct it, and it was green-lighted, made, and then released amid even madder developments than any in the film. You doubt me? Wait! A delegation of priests flown in from Notre Dame to see a rough cut of the picture in a screening room at Fox voiced no objections to the film except for one little thing. Near the end of the movie, there is a scene showing Notre Dame football players at an Arabian feast on the night before the big game and Notre Dame requested that a shot of a Notre Dame player holding a wine glass while watching a belly dancer be cut. The shot lasted only three or four seconds and was totally unnecessary, so no problem, right? *Wrong!* For I was told by J. Lee Thompson, who was in Zanuck's office and an eyewitness, that on hearing the news from Notre Dame, the head of the studio, the preeminently likeable Dickie Zanuck, rubbed his hands together in anticipatory glee over the prospect of a massive barrage of free publicity for the picture and declared, "Let's not cut it, guys! Maybe they'll sue us!" Well, indeed it wasn't cut and Notre Dame did sue, but instead of tons of free publicity, about a week before the film's scheduled opening, a judge in New York issued an injunction on its release as well as helpfully opining in his ruling that my screenplay was "ugly, vulgar and tawdry," descriptives I would later employ as the first names of three sisters in one of my later comic novels, but which also had the disastrous effect, on the day of the film's world premiere at the Criterion cinema on Broadway, of keeping anyone in New York City who had any respect for Notre Dame, Catholicism, motherhood, common decency, and the Irish people in general, from attending, while, instead, the turnout consisted almost entirely of every male low-life and sexual pervert in town who, after seeing the film and finding nothing indecent or prurient in it whatever, gave it *terrible word of mouth*!

Well, never mind all of that as I digress for just a moment with a word of some interest about the film's elfin, malmsey-nosed director, J. Lee Thompson, by entering Dr. Who's telephone box and leaping ahead to two excerpts concerning the character Burke Dennings in my novel to come, *The Exorcist*:

A slight, frail man in his fifties, he spoke with a charmingly broad British accent so clipped and precise that it lofted even

crudest obscenities to elegance, and when he drank, which was
most of the day, he seemed always on the verge of guffaw and
mightily struggling to retain his composure. ... Waiting on the
lawn at the base of the steps while the lights were warming,
Chris looked toward Dennings as he flung an obscenity at a
hapless grip and then visibly glowed with satisfaction. He
seemed to revel in his bad-boy eccentricity. Yet at a certain point
in his drinking, Chris knew, he could suddenly explode into
temper, and if it happened at three or four in the morning, he
was likely to telephone people in power and verbally abuse them
over trifling provocations. Chris remembered a studio chief
whose offense had consisted in remarking mildly at a screening
that the cuffs of Dennings' shirt looked slightly frayed, prompting
Dennings to awaken him the next morning at approximately

Ugly, vulgar, and tawdry.

3 A.M. to describe him as a "cunting boor" whose father, the founder of the studio, was "more than likely psychotic!" and had "fondled Judy Garland repeatedly" during the filming of *The Wizard of Oz.* Then on the following day he would pretend to amnesia and subtly radiate with pleasure when those he'd offended described in detail what he had done. Although, if it suited him, he would remember. Chris smiled and shook her head as she remembered him destroying his studio suite of offices in a gin-stoked, mindless rage, and how later, when confronted by the studio's head of production with an itemized bill and Polaroid photos of the wreckage, he'd sniffingly dismissed them as "Obvious fakes" since "the damage," he said, "was far, far worse than that!"

The only thing fictitious in this excerpt is the names. Dennings is Thompson, Chris is Shirley MacLaine, and the 3 a.m. call, the contents of which are word for word the absolute truth, was to Dickie Zanuck. Also word for word true is the dismissal by Thompson of the incriminating photos as "obvious fakes, the damage was far, far worse than that," for it was told to me by Thompson's co-perp in the matter, Shirley the Mac herself, as having happened during the filming of *What a Way to Go* in which she was starring with Thompson directing. So you see? Writing fiction is easy. All it takes is a very good memory. Meantime, now you know the kind of people that I chose to be my friends.

And, oh, yes, concerning that, there is more. Shirley, Thompson, and I made a pilgrimage to New York to pitch Darryl F. Zanuck, the iconic head of Twentieth Century Fox, to persuade him to make *John Goldfarb, Please Come Home!* We'd arrived the night before the meeting, scheduled for late afternoon the next day, and in the morning I asked Shirley if she'd do me a favor. Tommy Foley, my classmate and best friend at St. Stephen's Parochial School on East 28th Street, had developed Parkinson's Disease while late in his teens and was now a permanent resident in a hospital on Welfare

Island. Over coffee I told Shirley I was going to visit him and that I thought the greatest gift I could give him was a visit from a movie star. Now mind you, at that time I didn't know Shirley very well. Could she come with me, I dared to ask, as she lifted her coffee cup for a sip. Before it even got to her lips she said, "Sure." This was *also* a type I chose for a friend.

Tommy Foley and I hadn't seen one another in about twenty years and as we held out our arms to each other for a hug, we still addressed each other loudly as "Blatty!" and "Foley!" not Bill and Tommy, just as it was when we were kids, but, right after the hugs, "Miss Kubelik" a.k.a. "Irma La Douce/Sweet Charity" took over, sitting down on a bench next to Tommy. Her first question was, "What do you see yourself wanting to be?" and when he answered, "A writer," my heart sank even lower for him, but then it brightened as the mega-star proceeded at great length to ask questions about Tommy's family, his past life, his yearnings, his feelings about his present situation as if he were the single most important person to her on the planet which I believe that in that moment he actually was and in my mind there's still a glowing picture postcard of that moment.

Equally memorable was our meeting in the late afternoon with Zanuck. Encamped in a lavish suite in the Hotel Pierre while doing battle with the film censorship board over his upcoming film about Michelangelo, *The Agony and the Ecstasy*, he greeted us, the storied studio chief, lit cigar in hand, dressed in a colorfully embroidered silk kimono, standing behind a lengthy conference table covered with what appeared to be a blown up photograph of the ceiling of the Sistine Chapel with a sea of little red circles all over it. I don't recall him even saying "Hello," just "I'm going to whip those shitfaced censors! You hear? I'm going to knock them dead!" he declared, his eyes flashing defiantly under gold and white flecked bushy eyebrows as he waved his cigar hand over the photos with, "Did you know that there are ninety-seven pricks on the ceiling of the Sistine Chapel?!" When I recounted this to Peter Ustinov on the set of the "Wrong-Way" Goldfarb movie, his instant response was, "Not a record. The College of Cardinals has ninety-eight."

Shirley MacLaine, Writing Jerk, and Dick Crenna filming
John Goldfarb, Please Come Home!

That very night, the smokily dangerous and sexy looking movie star Robert Mitchum, long rumored to be entangled romantically with Shirley, joined us for celebratory drinks in her suite, after which we all set out to have dinner at Frankie and Johnnie's, but as the elevator door whooshed open on the hotel lobby floor we were greeted by Mitchum's wife, Dorothy, who immediately, and without uttering a word, reached up and, tightly gripping the ear of the terrifying portrayer of psychotic killers in *Cape Fear* and *The Night of the Hunter*, pulled him out of the elevator as if he were an errant schoolboy and never loosened her grip until she'd haled Mitchum out into the street where they stood alone and far to the side as they awaited a taxi while the three tipsy celebrants stood silent and apart from them as we awaited a separate cab. I noticed Dorothy had finally let go of Mitchum's ear. (Their marriage also lasted fifty-seven years until Mitchum's death.)

In an Epic New Movie, One Dame Beats Another

BY DAN JENKINS

When Hollywood shoots a whacky football film in the Mojave Desert, not even the Four Horsemen could save Notre Dame from a devastating half-back named Shirley MacLaine. With a script that calls for camels, harem girls, a lost U-2 pilot and the dousing of some real-life athletes with oily goo, it obviously matters not who wins or loses, but how Shirley plays

Our pilgrimage to Darryl F. Zanuck successfully ended—he'd approved the picture—there was to be yet another pilgrimage for Shirley, Thompson, and myself, one abounding in detail testing the limits of how far I could go in giving new meaning to the word "disgraceful." It had to do with the casting of the zany yet terrifying Arab potentate King Fawz of Fawzi Arabia. Trevor Howard, fresh off winning the Oscar for his portrayal of Captain Bligh in the remake of *Mutiny on the Bounty*, sent a cable to Thompson that read verbatim, "If you fail to cast me as Fawz, I will never speak to you again." Jack Lemmon, with whom we had talked about the role of John Goldfarb, also wanted the part of the king, as did George C. Scott who wanted to play both Goldfarb *and* King Fawz. However, Shirley M. had the *idee fixe* that it had to be Peter Ustinov, perhaps to give the film a touch of class, and thus it was that Thompson and I tagged along with Shirley to the Alpine town of Les Diablerets in Switzerland where the incomparable actor-author was holed up at a hotel with his wife Suzanne while he was writing a book. It is worth a brief mention, I suppose, that at an overnight stopover at a hotel fronting out to Lake Zurich, I found myself awake and dressed at about 5 a.m. and, looking out a window, espied in the distance our impish looking, frail, and diminutive British director. Bundled up in scarf and heavy coat against a bitter mid-February cold, he was briskly striding back toward the hotel along the otherwise deserted frozen lakefront walkway. Pleased and relieved to have someone to talk to over coffee at this hour, I took the elevator down to the lobby just in time to see Thompson shove open a door and then brusquely blow past me with an irritated mutter of, "Not a hooker in sight!" That, too, is in *The Exorcist* novel. But I digress.

When the "Beggars' Cup Trio" at last arrived in Les Diablerets, we found the Ustinovs had been invited to a modest little gathering in a chalet at the lower down town of Gstaad by Prince Rainier and his Princess Bride, the superstar and ravishing beauty, Grace Kelly. "Yes, of course, you must bring them," the gracious Prince Rainier told the Ustinovs. It wouldn't be long before I gave His Royal Highness much cause to regret it.

At Rainier's narrow chalet, present were not only the royals, but megastar David Niven so that, wide-eyed with starstruckonia and at the core of my soul still little Willie in the Brooklyn Paramount second balcony, I was instantly a nervous wreck, this triggering my customary mode of defense, namely getting as stupefyingly boxed as I could in the shortest possible time and from this there flowed the following "highlight reel": (1) While Prince Rainier, on an elevated platform, is performing his duties as host by changing vinyl records on an old-fashioned record player, I am dancing slow and very close with Princess Grace, and when a Sinatra song ends, I ask the prince to "Play that one again, would you please?" (2) While sitting at a table alone with Grace, we were overheard by a pixillated Suzanne Ustinov, who tells Peter the next morning that (a) I told Grace I could make her a star again, and that (b) I much preferred Peter Sellers for the part of King Fawz. "Oh, you couldn't have heard that correctly," Ustinov scoffed, to which Suzanne replied, "Oh, well, I heard very well, Peter. Really! I was right under their table!"

Source: Wikimedia Commons

Grace Kelly (for the millennials who don't recognize her name).

Shirley, J. Lee, and the Ustinovs left the party without me, leaving the Rainiers to have me escorted, if not hauled like a limp and sappily grinning top head on a totem pole, to another chalet and a room for the night. The next morning, while I was brunching with the princelings outdoors on roast pork, sauerkraut, and a nice Moselle wine, I would soon discover that at the same time Shirley and the Ustinovs were at breakfast in their hotel dining room pondering whether I was dead or alive and at which time Ustinov idly sketched on a dining room paper napkin a "Wanted Poster" featuring a portrait of me as a gaunt and goofy looking Arab sheik beneath the heading:

WANTED

HORIZONTAL OR VERTICAL

AL BIL EL BLAAAT

And you doubt me, right? Oh, well, of course. Yes, you think that I've made it all up, every word. Well, good! That's exactly what I want you to do so I can give you the proof and thus build trust in my recounting of certain supernatural events yet to come, and here it is, a ragged and unretouched photo of the actual Les Diablerets Hotel napkin with the Ustinov drawing on it:

And here, on page 108, although merely for your amusement, is another Ustinov napkin drawing made while we were filming the Notre Dame vs. Fawzi Arabia football game:

"Drivence Licing"
The "Lef Tum" "Rait Tum" pun is priceless.

By way of "Guilty with an Explanation," the latter being that my defense during episodes of "starstruckonia" is common to many other mortals as well, it was just such an event that led up to a moment of impossible dreaming. Shirley MacLaine had dispatched me to Tokyo along with her business manager Alan Lee in hopes I could come up with an idea for a movie comedy to star Shirley that could be shot in Japan. My very dear friend the actor Regis Toomey (*Meet John Doe, Guys and Dolls*) had given me the names and telephone number of two friends, an American couple living in Tokyo. On landing I called them and we were invited to dinner that night and on arriving found our hostess to be juiced to the eyeballs. And why? Because Judy Garland had been given the names of the same couple, had called them, and was shortly to arrive with her husband Mark and that, as they say, is the name of that tune. Meantime, as long as I'm here, my dears, I might as well tell you that when Judy arrived, our smashed hostess pointed to an armchair and commanded Judy to "Sit! Sit down!" Then when Judy returned from a bathroom pit stop, our host and hostess being elsewhere at the time, she breathed out a, "Whew! Now I know what's wrong with that woman: *you should see all the pills she takes*!" Dinner was not to be served at home, we then learned, but at a highly Americanized Hilton Hotel, so when we left the house ahead of our host and hostess, Judy grabbed me by the shoulder and said, "You come with me!" and in her limo she told us that she'd never before been to Japan, had only the one day there and was dying to sample Japanese culture, whereupon she turned her head to look out the rear window, saw the headlights of the host couple's car following at a distance, then turned to her driver and said, "Lose them!" We did. And there followed, led by old Tokyo hand Alan Lee, multiple visits to various Japanese eateries and clubs until finally, and because, as Lee later explained, Garland seemed bored beyond human imagination, he led us to the gay bar, a visitation I wouldn't trade for all the crunchy spicy tuna roll I could eat and where I watched in a state of total stun, my mouth agape in incredulity, as a Japanese "Gay Boy" in Geisha drag sitting opposite and close to Garland and looking straight into her eyes sang every verse of "Ovuh Da Lainbow." Yes. When we parted that night, I asked Judy to sign a fan that another "gay boy" geisha at the table named George had handed me, to which she answered, "Do you think I'm *crazy*?" Then, "Here!" after biting a piece out of the fan and handing it back to me with her lipsticked mouth imprinted upon it.

In the meantime, starstruckonia would uncoil itself yet again in an unexpected encounter with Barbra Streisand. It happened in 1971. *The Exorcist* novel had been sold to the movies and I was supine on the sofa of my rented A-frame dwelling close to Mulholland Drive trying to figure out how to do what I frankly believed at the time was the undoable, namely fashioning a screenplay from the novel that one could exhibit in theaters without being arrested and imprisoned for life when the telephone rang.

It was the answering service. The girl on the other end of the line could barely speak, she just stuttered for a moment before telling me in an awe-freighted voice, "It's *Barbara Streisand on the line*!" What? I'd never met or spoken to Streisand! Could it really be her?! I said, "Put her on," and it was. Who could mistake that voice! What followed was a brief and somewhat wandering conversation of which I can remember very little except that it wasn't exactly at the level of *My Dinner with Andre*, the highlight probably being Streisand's "Hey, that's some answering service you've got! They tell you who's calling before they connect?" Besides that, while I would love to be able to recount a somewhat racy conversation, the only other thing I clearly recollect is that she never explained why she was calling, although later I came to suspect that a matchmaking friend who knew everyone in town had given her my number and that she was feeling a little lonely in Malibu. *Yes, even Hud gets lonely,* I thought, remembering a line in a Paul Newman movie. It wouldn't have been surprising, really, since loneliness in beautiful and famous women was something I'd become well acquainted with while working the midnight to morning shift as a reservations agent for United Airlines in Los Angeles when a Jayne Mansfield, for example, would call at two or three in the morning to book a flight and would stay on the line with me forever, saying things like, "You have a nice voice," and "Yes," I was frequently tempted to respond, "I have *leading* man voice." As for Streisand, due mainly to my sharing of my answering service lady's shock and awe, nothing social ever came of her call. And yet through some circumstance that I cannot now recall, it was somehow arranged that I would meet with her in Las Vegas when she was performing there to discuss the possibility of her playing the mother in *The Exorcist*. And so it was that with a xerox copy of my yet to be published *The Exorcist* manuscript under my arm, on an appointed day I found her seated in a Las Vegas casino lounge surrounded by guards and associates and, true to my matchless Princess Grace form, I'd prepared myself for the meeting by downing any number of gin martinis so that when I shook her hand I must have gripped it so tightly that, judging from the terrified look on her face and the way she cringed and pulled, our little chat was to be briefer than the one we'd once hand on the phone as her guards closed around her even faster than the Secret Service had gotten to my mother when she met FDR.

So are we getting to know me yet? No? Well, here's more: When I chatted with host Ricardo Montalban at the first televising of a TV show called *Peoples' Choice for the Oscars*, I said, "How's Esther," meaning Esther Williams, the dazzling swim star who was married to Fernando Lamas, and for both of whom I had once cooked a Lebanese dinner. I am also guilty by association in that I was present at a mid-1960s gathering for the birthday of William Dozier, producer of the *Batman* television series, at the bar of the Beverly Hilton Hotel in L.A. Present and standing at the bar was the husky-voiced, whiskey-throated epitome of patrician, stand-offish bearing, the incomparable Tallulah Bankhead who had acted in several of the *Batman* episodes, while beside her, boxed beyond human imagining, was the diminutive Mickey Rooney, once the star of the ragingly popular Andy Hardy films along with Ann Rutherford as Polly Benedict, Andy Hardy's teenaged sweetheart, and now long married to Dozier. Not being personally acquainted with anyone present except for the Doziers, I was standing at the bar, within earshot of Rooney and Bankhead, when I overheard Rooney saying, "You know, Tallulah, I'd really love to fuck you," and then Tallulah, her ivory cigarette holder held aloft in her hand, looked down haughtily at Andy Hardy and replied, "Well, if you do and I ever find out about it...."

Ah, the rich and ever entertaining *La Dolce Vita* that I thought I was living, rubbing elbows with the likes of Rita Hayworth and Gary Cooper or having Johnny Weissmuller, the best and most famed of the movie Tarzans, explaining to me in great and very proud detail why his swimming pool franchise was vastly superior to Esther Williams. And breathes there a soul so dead who will deny that I have lived a life after learning that at a dinner party at the home of a friend and our only living motion picture superstar, Kirk Douglas, I overheard Jimmy Stewart telling him in his inimitable, quavery Midwestern drawl, "I-I-I just don't want to narrate a documentary about raccoons"? Although let me be clear: these contacts were mostly by-products of my work, for having become known to unexpectedly say upsetting things like "God" and "Don't you think you should stop that?" in social situations, I soon became as desirable at dinner party tables as a blood-soaked Banquo's ghost, a point driven home to me one sunny day in May by my friend the aforementioned Mr. Douglas, who appeared at my front door dressed for tennis and carrying a racquet. "Bill, hi!! No, I'm not coming in," he said. "I just wanted to thank you for your incessant cards and phone calls and letters," he went on, wryly chiding me for not having been in touch with him for a while. Then he leaned forward, embracing me tightly and I listened to Spartacus quietly growling into my ear, "Bill! Bill! Nobody likes us! We must *cling* to one another!"

Ah, well, there are so many more wondrous tales I could tell about my Hollywood career. Near the end of the science-fiction movie *Blade Runner,* the dying leader of the artificial humans called "replicants," his head bent low and breathing his last, reminisces, "I've seen things you people wouldn't believe…starships on fire off the shoulder of Orion…" My story is much the same. But aware of your testiness and infantile impatience when not being *constantly* entertained, I intend to be judicious and recount for you only a few more special incidents that I think might bring a smile to your jaded lips while at the same time building your confidence that I am not someone easily given to seeing St. Francis of Assisi preaching to the birds in my pepperoni pizza, or one given to retailing colorful "dish" such as Shirley MacLaine describing for me how at the end of a White House visit President John F. Kennedy chased her around her waiting limo. I am not that sort of person.

Considering what very few additional incidents best reveal precisely the sort of person I actually am, and this get us so much closer to discussing my son Peter and life after death, there doe swim numbingly to mind, and with dizzying speed, my meeting in the squeeze of August heat with the legendary Russian ballet dancer Rudolph Nureyev in an airport lounge in St. Louis, Missouri, with the aim of persuading him to co-star with the

Smothers Brothers in a movie I had written. With me was the film's producer, Malcolm Stuart, and on the plastic tabletop in front of me was my
three-page typed synopsis of the movie's plot and characters that I'd
brought for Nureyev to read right during the one-hour flight layover that
was the only time he had available to meet with us. Then disaster struck
as, in my excitement at being in Nureyev's presence, I suppose, I tipped
over my styrofoam cup of coffee, drenching the synopsis, while *Shit! Shit!*
Shit!" and "*Why me, God? Why? Why me?*" were my hysterical, puling
thoughts as I frenziedly blotted at the pages with a paper napkin before
jumping up and rushing them to a rest room where I held them under the
heated airflow of a hand-dryer, then rushed back toward the table until I
turned a corner and was in sight of the table, at which point I stopped dead
in my tracks and, with chin tilted slightly upward, assumed a very slow
and carefree walk and manner, even looking around as if casually taking
in the sights of the airport terminal in a hopelessly doomed if not ludicrous
effort to convey to Nureyev a sense of unruffled aplomb. As I at last
reached the table and seated myself, I handed him the blotched and still
faintly damp pages of my synopsis, which he greeted with twinkly eyes
and a bemused, almost mischievous, dimpled little smile that were a perfect match for his puckish viz. That he didn't do the picture has zero
importance. No, the lesson here is character: the incredible grit, daring,
and resourcefulness of a young writer, the son of impoverished Lebanese
immigrants who, facing intense, if not borderline unbearable psychological pressure, saved from extinction the plot and character notes for
"*And They Said That Nijinsky Was Crazy.*"

Then there was the time that, invited to lunch at the home of movie star
Tippi Hedren for the purpose of meeting Gloria Steinem, as four of us—
including Tippi's husband who for some reason was raising lions and tigers
in their Sherman Oaks home—sat sedately at a card table set up for lunch
while above us behind a balustrade a four-hundred-pound lion named
"Neil" was stretched out motionless while quietly observing us until, without provocation, or as some sort of lion joke, perhaps, he suddenly decided to

leap gracefully over the balustrade, sending dishes and wine glasses clattering to the floor as he landed on our table with a heavy grace and then quietly looked from one to the other of us with an expression that seemed to say, "So?" I reached up a hand to pet him.

Neil contemplating his next move.
Ditto.

Equally memorable, I suppose, was that Friday in New York in the winter of 1973 where after a day of filming *The Exorcist*, director Billy Friedkin and I found a drink at the Oak Bar of the Plaza Hotel in Manhattan where Billy voiced concern that Ellen Burstyn, in the role of the mother of the possessed Regan MacNeil, was expressing anxiety about the start of the exorcism sequence which was scheduled to begin on Monday morning with a scene in which Burstyn would answer the doorbell in her rental home in Georgetown to find standing there a priest who on

taking off his hat would reveal him to be the great Swedish actor Max
Von Sydow. "Mrs. MacNeil," he would say, "I'm Father Merrin." "Wish I
knew how to relax her," Billy said with concern, to which I responded
that I thought I knew a way, which was to surprise Ellen and give her an
angst-dissolving laugh to find that when Merrin lifts off his hat he's
revealed to be not Von Sydow but Joe Fretwell, our costume designer who
had a southern drawl even deeper than Dixie. Friedkin shook his head.
"No, not Fretwell," he said; "Groucho Marx." My eyebrows lifted.
"Groucho?" I said. "Billy, Groucho's in town. He's staying at The Sherry.
We're friends. Should I ask him if he'd do it, Billy? Would you shoot it?"
"Yes. Absolutely." And so on Sunday I found myself in a meeting with
Groucho in the Russian Tea Room. I'd first met him when I was a con-
testant on his weekly quiz show *You Bet Your Life* at which time time I
was posing as a son of King Saud of Saudi Arabia, "Prince Xairallah el
aswad el Xeer," which is another whole story for some other time and
which I may or may not get back to. We'll see. In the meantime, on
Groucho's show I had not only answered the "Big Jackpot Question" but
had also uttered "The Secret Word," which triggered a plastic duck suspended by wires to drop down from above while gripping in its beak a
placard on which was printed the "word." And so it came to pass that,
over blinis and tea, my "relax Ellen Burstyn" script expanded far beyond
just surprising Ellen Burstyn when she answers the doorbell and finds
herself face to face with Groucho Marx, as I decided that on yet another
shot, Groucho, in full Jesuit attire, would enter the possessed child Regan's
bedroom whereupon Linda Blair's stunt double, in full demon makeup
and with both her wrists bound to the padded posts of a four-poster bed,
would greet him by shouting out in an electronically distorted, deep
demonic voice, the single most obscene word in the English language—
eight letters, starts with "c"—whereupon the duck would drop down
disclosing it to be the "secret word." The remainder of the plan, of which
Groucho had no knowledge, was that Friedkin and I would wait until we
knew all the Warner Brothers studio executives in Burbank had seen the

shots along with that day's "dailies," at which point our telephone operator was instructed not to take their calls for the rest of the week.

The Prince on *You Bet Your Life* struggling to find the answer to
"Where are the Egyptian pyramids located?"

The Prince about to turn to partner for the answer to
"How long have you been here in Los Angeles, Your Highness?"

There. That's enough. And so now as we bid farewell to my Tinseltown saga, it is Kirk Douglas who stars in a final and fittingly hilarious dismal anecdote that encapsulates my Tinseltown days. I was at home watching TV as Kirk was interviewing Zero Mostel at the world premiere of *The Great Bank Robbery*, a comedy I had written and in which Mostel starred, when, lowering my face into both my hands I quietly groaned after I'd heard Kirk say enthusiastically, "You know, I read the script of this movie! It's really great," and Mostel raised an eyebrow as he asked with an honest and innocent perplexity, "It *is?*"

TEN

I don't intend to do much talking about *The Exorcist*. It's been over forty years now of answering questions about it and I'm frankly pretty tired of being hauled out of my burrow every year at Halloween like some demonic Punxsutawney Phil. And yet it is *The Exorcist* that's at the heart of my tale of that hidden programmer I refer to as Providence and to which I now return.

And so it happened that in 1968, after a nice run of motion picture comedies based on my screenplays, the market for comic films went suddenly dead. What to do? Film, and not books, had been my source of income, and my thoughts turned to trying my hand at a play. One idea that I had was about God and the Devil holding peace talks at 3 a.m. in the Carnegie Deli, while another concept was about two Israeli agents named Hammacher and Schlemmer who have been hunting for Martin Bormann together for thirty years and on the anniversary of the day their mission started one of them has forgotten. But lacking the confidence to start writing either one, I found myself in a space where I was continuing to brood, and now much more clearly and with a firmer intent, about that case of possession and exorcism that I'd heard about in theology class while a junior at Georgetown University in the winter of 1949. Running up to that moment I had attended a campus lecture by a visiting priest about a "miraculous" fall of rose petals bearing the image of the Blessed Virgin Mary at Lipa, in the Philippines, whenever three young girls went into rapture and claimed to see and hear her. The priest had brought along with him a windowed display of some three dozen of these petals and at the end of his lecture we formed a queue to take turns at examining them up close. I'll never forget it: to my left and viewing the display just ahead of me was a tubby classmate, "Wowie" Carter, who having taken an eye-widening look at the Virgin Mary's very clearly defined and unambiguous imprint on the rose petals, turned to me with wide and shining eyes and excitedly exclaimed, "Well, what are we waiting for?!!"—a pronouncement whose meaning I puzzled over for days before narrowing it down to two possibilities, these being (1) "This is proof our faith is true, so now let's run out into the world and evangelize!" or (2) "This is proof our faith is true, so let's give all of our earthly possessions to the poor, quit drinking, give up girls, and enter the priesthood." I settled on Interpretation One as the more plausible, so when the following year I heard in class about an ongoing case of possession and exorcism occurring somewhere in the greater nabe, it immediately struck me that a strengthening of faith à la "Wowie" Carter would be even far more powerful if that case could be extensively researched and found to be genuine, and over the coming years, although admittedly distantly and dimly, that apostolic intent abided. That in Los Angeles in the summer of 1968 I finally decided to act upon it was for a reason lacking even the faintest blush of the transcendent. As I've mentioned, with comedy films being out of vogue I had little else to do besides showing up weekly at the Van Nuys Unemployment Office. Want to hear how God works in "mysterious ways"? Try this: the proximate trigger that suddenly intensified my resolve to evangelize and bolster faith was the day I was standing in the unemployment line with my eyes flared wide and a recidivist spasm shuddering up my back after spotting my screenwriting agent in the third line down from mine. Is this honest enough for you? Good. But much less good was the publishing world's reception of my notion for a book about demonic possession, which elicited a level of interest perhaps equal to that of a dying sparrow in a last meal offer of a hot fudge sundae with sprinkles although a moment of hopeless hope did flicker while I was in London writing *A Shot in the Dark* for Blake Edwards. I told Blake about my idea, offered him 100 percent of the movie rights in exchange for enough cash to keep me afloat for up to a year, and he accepted but with one condition. On completion of the first draft screenplay, I had been assigned the task of returning to Los Angeles and offering the role of the female lead to my friend Shirley MacLaine, and while there I was to tell my idea for a novel of possession to Blake's partner, the producer Marty Jurow, for his approval. That day at last came. Shirley turned down the part: "I want to play Inspector Clouseau," she joked, and off I was to a meeting with Jurow at his office where, as the producer and I sat in facing overstuffed chairs, I did a lengthy and passionate Scheherazade about my exorcism novel. Jurow's reaction? He looked down at my feet and said, "Bill, where did you get those shoes?" And so it was that, with all gates on the novel slammed shut, one late night on September 23, 1968, I decided to see if I could turn my idea into a movie script. I got a page and a half into it, with Damien Karras making a confession, and that's as far as I had gotten when the telephone rang. It was the family doctor. Mama had passed away.

I put down the telephone receiver, stunned and staring off into space. It was as if a mountain had suddenly disappeared from the horizon. I didn't cry. Not then. I was dazed. Nothing was real. I drove to the Briarwood Convalescent Home nearby on Ventura Boulevard. The men from the mortuary were there. The last time I'd seen her a few days before, Mama was sitting in Briarwood courtyard and applying lipstick and she stared at the soda-pop machine refiller, a tall sixtyish good-looking Swede on whom she had a crush. Now she was staring up at me through dulled and sightless eyes. I looked down at her impassively, then leaned over and kissed her forehead as I had, thank God, just a week before after telling her how wonderful a mother she had been to me and how much I loved her and she'd said, "Willie, you very good boy." Around her neck were two religious medals bearing the imprint of the Blessed Virgin Mary. One was small, round, and coppery and largely covered with greenish mold because apparently she never took it off. The other medal was of a silvery color. I took it off, put it around my neck, then watched as the morticians wrapped her in a white sheet, placed her in their ambulance, and drove off. I returned to the guest house, removed the seal from a fifth of vodka, took it out to the deck with me, sat down, looked up at the stars and then burst into convulsive sobbing and tears that never abated until the dawn when not a drop of the vodka remained. There'd been a moment in that dark of night when no sooner than seconds after I'd cried out aloud for angels to come carry my mother to a place of eternal happiness, I'd seen an enormous white light slowly drifting across the sky. It was probably the vodka. There was a telescope of sorts on the porch but I was too drunk to properly focus it on the light. And then it was gone. Like the light within me. Even when I'd visit her in the convalescent home, I could still crack Mama up by saying, "I gonna pass dat'a truck!" I had lost that laughter forever.

Or so I then believed.

At the mortuary days later, my brother Moe called out loudly, "You showed them, Mama!" Amen. She is buried at San Fernando Missionary Cemetery a few yards from a statue of the Blessed Virgin Mary to whom she was deeply devoted, and not far from the gravesite of Richie Valens. On her tombstone are the words, "LOVE. COURAGE."

I grieved for a thousand years.

"Love. Courage."

ELEVEN

Burton Wohl is a talented novelist and screenplay writer whom I'd met while he was working for producer Bill Bloom on a movie adaptation of his novel *A Cold Wind in August* at the very same time that I was writing *The Man from the Diners' Club*. I came to like him very much in general, and for two specific things in particular. The first was his reaction to losing a Scrabble challenge to me, which was to turn aside and airily dismiss my word as "Poor usage." The other was the time we were both ensconced at the Plaza Hotel in New York, each of us developing separate screenplays for Malcolm Stuart, a producer and former agent with a reputation for extreme frugality that survived unblemished, if not deepened, when he picked up a phone in one of our rooms where Wohl and I had both ordered lunch, hung it up with a scowl, and then turned to inform us bitterly, "Your ten dollar hamburgers are here." One early evening when the producer and I were having a dinner—the "Five O'Clock Special" at Stuart's suggestion—in a virtually empty Oak Room,

Wohl, having spotted us from afar, came happily bounding up to our table, an action followed instantly by the sound of a number of waiters' feet stampeding to the spot and then Wohl being sternly ordered to leave the room "immediately" because he wasn't wearing a tie. What followed was a Marx Brothers movie. Pointing to a heavyset diner hunched over his meal at a nearby table, "What about *that* gentleman?" Wohl inquired of the leader of the waiters. "What gentleman, sir?" "That very *large* one right over there," Wohl replied. The person Wohl was pointing at was wearing a skimpy string tie. He was also Orson Welles. And suddenly, magically, the waiters accosting Wohl looked off as if suddenly summoned to some non-existent duty in a distant corner of the room—one even gasped, "My God! *No!*" as he looked off in that direction—and then off the waiters fled none knows whither and it was in that moment that my bond of friendship with Wohl deepened to the point of becoming unbreakable. However the friendship was sorely tested when in late December 1968 he invited me to his home in the hills of Sherman Oaks for a New Year's Eve party, at which I shook my head slowly and told him, "No. No, I never go to New Year's Eve parties anymore. True. Not in almost twenty years because almost always," I explained, "at the stroke of midnight there's always some drunken asshole doing something way out of line and I'm done with all that," although not mentioned was the fact that the drunken asshole referred to was usually me. But "Come on, it's just a few friends, Bill," Wohl persisted. "You can leave before midnight, or whenever, okay?"

I was about to say no again but there was something in his voice and in his stare, and so I crumbled and attended the party where within a short time, sitting on a hassock very close and facing me was a man with a dark and sweeping moustache that would have made him a credible entry in a Pancho Villa look-alike contest. He was hunched over, a tall drink cupped in his hands, and asked me, "So what are you working on, Bill?" He would turn out to be Marc Jaffe, chief of the editorial department at Bantam Books. I'd never met him before. He must have known me, I guessed, from my comic novels and I hesitated, wondering whether or not to risk loss of reputation as a humorist, thus losing a potential publisher, by telling him about my idea for a book about demonic possession, but then took a breath and plunged recklessly ahead. It took only a minute or two, because that's all I really knew about the book: no characters, no plot, just possession. When I'd finished, Jaffe nodded, saying, "I'll publish that." I got happily juiced and stayed at the party past midnight without incident. Two miracles back to back.

And so it came about that in a two room clapboard guest house of a home in the hills of Encino formerly owned by Angela Lansbury, and with only coffee and cigarettes as companions, I settled in to writing *The Exorcist* from fourteen to sixteen hours a day *every* day and through the night until dawn, which included what I think of as "dream time" when the contents of my unconscious mind—or so I believe—were transparent and available to me, which is why, I suppose, that whenever I have occasion to read a passage from the novel today I am sometimes given to wondering who wrote it. Never mind. And so still without a plot and praying fervently that I wouldn't wind up painting myself into a corner, I simply put my head down and doggedly moved forward from chapter to chapter making sure that nothing ahead contradicted what had come before, and maybe that was a blessing, as I've since come to speculate that not having a strict outline might have the advantage of keeping the mind open for surprising and unanticipated developments. For example, I had originally intended to utilize the character of the director Burke Dennings for comic relief, and still vividly remember looking up in surprise as, lifting my fingers from the keyboard of my pale green IBM Selectric, I softly uttered, "Jesus! Burke Dennings is going to get killed!" I was once told by another writer, the son of Pulitzer Prize–winning playwright Marc Connelly, the author of *Green Pastures*, "You know, my characters sometimes take over and they lead me down dark alleyways and mug me," and when he asked if that was often my experience, my truthful answer was, "No. If I stop telling them what to do and say for even a second they just stand there with their jaws agape staring at me droopy-eyed and looking stupid." The case of Burke Dennings remains the lone exception.

In about nine months the novel was finished. Bantam sold hardcover rights to Harper and Row, and despite good reviews, a heavy advertising budget, plus appearances on *The Tonight Show* with Johnny Carson, *The David Frost Show, The Phil Donahue Show*, the Mike Douglas and Merv Griffin shows, as well as a twenty-six city book tour in which I was interviewed between ten and fifteen times a day, *The Exorcist* was a resounding sales disaster. No one—and I absolutely do mean *no* one—was buying the book, and my arrivals in city after city replicated that of Cleveland, the first one I visited, where the Harper salesman, with a copy of the novel with my photo on the back to help him identify me, greeted me at the bottom of the ramp as I debarked from the plane with, "Hi! Mr. Blatty? I'm the Harper sales rep. My Company just returned all one hundred copies of your book," and it wouldn't be long before the Harper salesmen didn't even need to rely on my photo for identification, they just watched for the most depressed-looking male of my age to come slouching down the ramp.

What finally at first seemed to lift my spirits occurred when I hit Las Vegas where a thinned down interview schedule gave me an hour or so for a drink and some gambling in the Desert Inn casino and where I was sitting at a blackjack table when a bellhop approached, asked if I were "Mr. Blatty," and then informed me that Elvis Presley wished to invite me to his suite! After security and paramedics had been called and I became conscious of the slapping at my face and the smelling salts held under my nose, I was helped—oh, well, half-carried—up to the "King's" suite where present were Presley, his pretty little wife Priscilla, and Presley's karate instructor. My instant impression of "The King" was that he was a humble innocent. He *introduced himself!* And then immediately took me to his bedroom to proudly point out a photo that he'd hung on the wall of himself and President Richard Nixon. But it was when we returned to the living room that I would finally come to realize why Elvis wanted to meet me, for, as it turned out, the boy was a "seeker." Barely a minute later, and without preamble, he had us standing close up to one another, face within inches of face, as he read aloud to me his every personally underlined passage in each of a stack of five or six books about theology and metaphysics. It took well over half an hour, and when it ended, Elvis and the instructor, who would one day hie himself off with the fair Priscilla, changed into flowing white karate outfits and put on an exhibition in which Elvis kicked the living crap out of the instructor. And then it came. As I was leaving, standing with the door partly open, I asked Elvis if he'd like me to sign his copy of *The Exorcist*.

"I didn't buy one," he said. "I saw you on TV."

Back in New York at the end of the tour, a doggedly, blindly optimistic Harper sales rep took me to B. Altman's department store to autograph copies of my novel. "I'm scenting something in the air," he said to me as we were approaching the entrance to the building. What he was scenting, it turned out, was something like the smoke from three-day-old napalm for once inside the store, we were greeted by a young salesgirl who asked us to wait while she consulted with the book department manager, then returned to inform us that I couldn't sign the book, and when "Why not?" the Harper rep asked her she replied a touch pissily, "Because Mr. Hoskins says that then we wouldn't be able to return them."

The writing was on the wall, on the sidewalks, and even at Bickford's, the McDonald's of its day, where at noon the same day I found it easy to suspect that the acned young waiter staring at me oddly from behind the counter was weighing whether or not to deny me service. And then later that day Harper added grievous insult to psychic injury by offering me any number of copies of the novel at a cost of only fifty cents apiece, betraying clearly they must have thought me a total idiot!

Actually, they were kind. They assigned a copy editor, a young woman, to treat me to a farewell lunch at The Four Seasons, which in a way, I suppose, brings up the subject of the supernatural somewhat earlier than I had planned, inasmuch as the venue I actually deserved was either The Automat or Bickford's and I will always believe that what happened next was surely by the hand of Providence, if not an outright miracle, plain or with hash browns on the side. Here's what happened. The Harper girl and I had barely been seated when a waiter brought a telephone to the table. A call for the Harper rep. She picked it up, listened, then, covering the mouthpiece of the phone with her hand, she quickly shot at me, "*The Dick Cavett Show* wants you at their studio right away!" I thought, *What*?! Yes, I'd auditioned for the *Cavett Show* weeks before, at the end of which the girl who had interviewed me told me, "Mr. Blatty, I find all of this kind of stuff fascinating, but please don't get your hopes up: Dick is death on the supernatural." What had happened now to change that disposition was that one of the show's prime guests had suddenly fallen ill, and with a cold and heartless prayer of thanksgiving on my lips, I threw down my napkin, raced out of The Four Seasons and then ran all the way to the studio where the show was being taped, went into makeup, and then finally took a seat in the Green Room to await the customarily meager "Author's Spot" which was always the last five minutes of the show. But then I learned how cold-bloodedly ruthless Providence can be in achieving its ends. The first guest, Keefe Brasselle, who was starring in the Broadway hit play *Sleuth*, lasted just one segment before getting the hook for reasons which even back then were not clear to me, except that the guest to follow him, a surefire dynamite interviewee, was the loquacious and always colorfully entertaining actor Robert Shaw. However, no sooner had Shaw been introduced than he wasted no time in assuring the television-viewing world at large that he was juiced to the very eyebrows, if not totally beyond the belief of even saints, and fearing, no doubt, that in this state the unpredictable actor was fully capable of saying or doing virtually anything one can imagine as well as, and more to the point, what one would make novenas *not* to imagine, the show gave Shaw the hook as well. And then out I came—the show's only other guest—to a butt-wiggling, charmingly smirky introduction in which Cavett made it clear that he had not read my book and with the strong implication that he doubtless never would. "Oh, well okay, then, may I tell you about it?" I asked, the answer to which found me doing a

forty-one-minute monologue about the novel interrupted only by com-
mercials and a single question: Do you believe in the existence of Satan?
My answer, which I cannot remember, must have been aces back to back
for the following week while at Kennedy Airport and about to fly home
in total misery, funk, and dejection, I picked up a copy of *Time* magazine
at an airport shop, masochistically flipped to the books bestseller list for
the purpose of luring me into soaking it in my spit along with some scath-
ing Lebanese invective, such as "The milk of your mother was wasted!"
while instead I nearly "lost it" as with trembling hands and a quivering
jaw and apparently possessed by Omer Aga, that almond farmer in Iraq,
I began babbling things like *manongaheela koo biki* and *pasta kostelanetz*
as with an almost stupefying disbelief I saw that on the fiction list my novel
was number four! Three weeks later it was number one on the *New York
Times* hardcover fiction list where some kindly but possibly besotted
patron saint, or maybe chain novenas said by all our old landlords in hopes
I would pay them the owed back rent, kept it on the list for fifty-seven
straight weeks, seventeen at number one!

There's more: Just prior to its publication, film rights to the novel
were offered to every major movie studio and fly-by-night film production company in town. I only wish I had kept the letters of rejection—all
of them printed form letters—for I could easily have papered the walls
of my den with them. That the novel at last became a film was only—
and incredibly—because a "hot" producer, Paul Monash, the creator of
Peyton Place and fresh off the success of *Butch Cassidy and the Sundance
Kid*, resubmitted it to Warner Brothers. Rather than the story department evaluating it, this time it was read by John Calley, the studio's
affable and talented vice president for creative affairs. As Calley once
related the tale to me, the reason the novel would become a film was all
because of an obedient German Shepherd dog. He was reading the novel,
Calley said, while alone and abed in his hillside home late at night when
he began to be spooked by the soft scratching sounds of tree branches
brushing over his roof in a gentle wind, so much so that he called for his

German Shepherd to get up on the bed with him. But the dog, having long been forbidden to get on the bed under threat of brutal beatings and having his name changed to "Toto," resisted, whereupon Calley got out of bed and attempted to drag it, whining and whimpering and with its dug-in claws tearing scratches into the polished heart-pine floor, into bed with him, when suddenly, Calley told me, he stopped his efforts and looked up and into space with the realization, as he put it, *"We've got to make this!"*

In 1974, on the night of the Academy Awards, Jason Miller, the film's Father Karras, shared a limo that took us to the event. Jason was to present the award for Best Screenplay based on another work, and knowing there would be a camera on the nominees, I said, "Jason, for *God's* sake, when you open the envelope (with the name of the winner), give me a heads-up so the camera doesn't catch me with a look of total depression if it isn't me. If it's me, just smile before you announce it." There were two Academy Awards that night, one in which I lost and the one in which I won, because if Jason smiled when he saw the winner's name, I didn't see it and as I turned my head to speak to the person seated next to me, shamelessly feigning to be a gracious loser and ready to loudly applaud the winner while inwardly cursing his very name, I was stunned to hear my name, at which point I believe I left my body for a moment; then on stage as I held the Oscar statuette, silently thanking God and publicly thanking William Bloom, who had taught me how to write a screenplay, director Billy Friedkin, the Academy, and my parents who come to America on a cattle boat, life held the sweetness of joyful surprise, but as my gaze was searching the seats down in front and below me, I would have given the Oscar and all I owned or ever dreamed of having to hear Mama say "That's him! That's my Willie! That's my boy!"

And now may we ever so quietly and dispassionately review the mad chain of "coincidences" leading to this wildly improbable event? I swear to you, it boggles the mind!

1. What if one of the guests on *The Dick Cavett Show* hadn't dropped out much sooner than the very last minute so that Cavett, who is hostile to *The Exorcist*'s subject matter, could have the time to dial around for a more fitting replacement?

2. What if I'd been in a taxi or in The Four Seasons men's room when Harper telephoned its rep?

3. What if not one but *two* of the *Cavett Show*'s star guests hadn't gotten the hook after just one segment?

4. What if I hadn't broken a twenty-year tradition of not attending New Year's Eve parties by attending Burton Wohl's?

5. What if Bantam chief editor Marc Jaffe hadn't been present at the party?

6. What if I hadn't mysteriously—and still unaccountably—won that scholarship to Georgetown so that I would never have heard about the 1949 case of demonic possession in a junior year New Testament class?

7. What if Neil Sullivan, who taught theology at Georgetown, had not eaten a second helping of Mama's Thanksgiving luncheon, prompting Mama's determination that I was "gonna go Georgetown," or worse, had picked at his food?

If this wasn't Providence at work, what was it?

Capping the point with a short-handled sledgehammer was the mother of my friend, the famed "insult comedian" Don Rickles. One night I was a guest on the *The Tonight Show* when Rickles was filling in as guest host for Johnny Carson. Don and I had known one another ever since my comedy screenwriting days when I had written two TV series pilot episodes in which Don was the star, one called "Plotkin Prison, We Love You"—see how honest I'm being?—and the other, "Which Way to Mecca, Jack?" in which Don was to play a kind of Sergeant Bilko in the desert, a royal con man reduced to that state by being the only Arabian potentate without a single drop of oil in his kingdom. Neither show ever made it to air, and when he heard I'd arrived at the studio, Don leaped out of his makeup chair to come flying down the corridor, his green smock still on and flapping, until he was nose to nose with me, and with his wicked, shining eyes glaring up at me almost tauntingly, he said, "Blatty!" No "Hello, how've you been?" Just "Blatty! I called my mother in Florida this morning and I said to her, 'Mama, guess who's on the show with me tonight?' and she says to me, 'Who, Don?' And 'Bill Blatty!' I tell her and my mother says, 'Why?', then when I say to her, 'Bill wrote *The Exorcist*!' my mother said, '*How*??!!'"

Well, all right. I've now given you enough information about myself, my background, my character, my failings, my quirks and odd quiddities, for you to trust both my word and my ability to see and hear and then report without color of subjectivity whatever this quirky material universe might have chosen to show me of itself. And so, do you? Do you trust me to tell you the absolute truth? If your answer is yes, turn the page.

PART THREE

Is the Universe a Thought in the Mind of God?

Quantum Physics has shown us that the
clockwork, mechanistic universe of 19th
century materialism was the greatest
superstition of its age.

—Arthur Koestler

TWELVE

I t was the renowned British physicist Sir James Jeans who, after years of attempting to unify all of the laws of matter in a single coherent theory, at the last decided that the only way in which that could be done was by assuming the material universe and everything in it were thoughts in the mind of God, while in the decades since then the quantum physicists have been telling us that there are no such things as things, there are only processes, and that matter is a kind of illusion. We live in a universe, they say, in which electrons can travel from a point in space to another point millions of miles away without traversing the space in between; that a positron is an electron that is traveling backwards in time; that in any two-particle system, changing the charge of one of the particles instantly changes the charge of the other even if the particles are several light-years apart; and that nothing really exists until it is observed. And so I ask: In a universe such as this, should there really be any such thing as surprise?

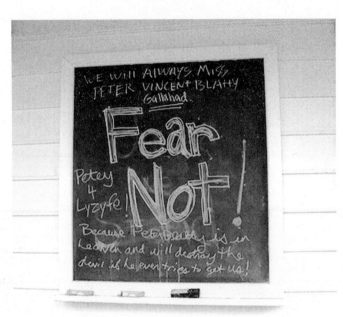

Blackboard elegy for Peter by grieving young friends.
"Peter Blatty is in heaven and will destroy the devil if he ever tries to get us!"

Before beaming you up into what I intend to be a further and more trying test of your trust in my word, if not of my sanity, I just want to get a few things straight, for if on reading Part Three you are hesitant to believe, you might be even more incredulous at the contents of Part Four and, to put it frankly to you, Scarlet, a bit foolish to even go there. For now, though, let's not buy trouble. This report, unembellished by smiling, ingratiating prose, will be brief, if not terse, and as devoid of even the slightest insinuation that the events here reported have anything whatever to do with so-called supernatural forces. Herewith then, in roughly chronological order are, as *Dragnet*'s Sergeant Friday would have put it, "The facts, ma'am, just the facts."

INCIDENT #1

Should you suspect that "The Strange Case of 059," or anything of that nature to come, are products of my imagination, it is with the utmost humility, if not shame, that I am forced to confess that this vaunted faculty of mine was totally missing in action from 1933 or thereabouts, until sometime late in 1969 when I was visiting a former college classmate and professor at the Georgetown University School of Law, Dick Gordon, at his home in Washington, D.C., where I was negotiating by long distance telephone an option agreement for the film rights to *The Exorcist*. Glued to a chair beside an end table on which rested a package of Marlboro cigarettes, a Zippo lighter, and the center of my nervous attention all that day—a cream-colored telephone receiver—when suddenly it rang, and as I was reflexively reaching for the cigarette pack and the Zippo, the telephone receiver rose up off its base and clattered to the end-table top. I picked up the phone, spoke a hollow "Hello" worthy of Boris Karloff saying "Carruthers" or "carotid artery" and found myself talking—for perhaps the fifth time that day—to Bill Tennant, the movie agent on the other side of the deal. Dick Gordon was in the room all through the mini levitation and when I'd hung up the phone on the agent, I said, "Dick, did you *see* what the phone just did?" He nodded, then said almost inaudibly, "Yes." Lawyers approach everything with classic CYA. We briefly chatted about it, then I called the telephone company and asked to speak to a phone company engineer who then came on the line and listened to my account of events, which ended with my asking whether some electrical force generated by the ringing of the phone might have caused it to seemingly "fly off its base." His reply in the negative ended with the words, "Our telephones do not fly," and when I told him I was speaking of a "Princess" phone I heard a click quickly followed by an unamused dial tone.

INCIDENT #2

Time: the early 1970s after the release of *The Exorcist* film. Place: the living room of the comedian Richard Pryor's home in the hills above

Sunset Boulevard. The occasion: a dinner party. One of the gentlest, truly innocent, and wounded souls I have ever met, I had come to know Richard when I was thinking of casting him in my film, *The Ninth Configuration*. Now to fully appreciate the "thing that was to happen," you have to picture me sitting with my wife on a little "love seat" directly in front of a massive fire pit, above it an enormous oil painting measuring roughly five feet wide and six tall, while behind us, hidden from our sight, were the other guests, among them Sidney Poitier and his wife Joanna. After dinner we were all having coffee when, just as Richard appeared before us with sugar and cream on a silver tray, we were jolted by a sudden shattering sound as the massive painting above the fire pit came crashing to the ground, and in the apprehensive, breath-holding hush that ensued, I felt everyone's stare on the back of my head, a phenomenon probably due to it being widely known that in one of my guest appearances to discuss *The Exorcist* on *The Tonight Show* with Johnny Carson, for the first time in the show's history they lost sound, while in yet another appearance, and again for the first time in the show's history, they lost picture, not to mention some published nonsense about marble coffee tables splitting in half and pictures falling off walls when I appeared on TV, all of this, like stories of paranormal phenomena on the set of *The Exorcist*, being a steaming crock of hot peaches started by *Newsweek*, if not the Warner Brothers publicity department whom I'm convinced hired actresses dressed as nuns to stand in front of the downtown London theater exhibiting the film and sprinkle holy water on anyone buying a ticket, and for moments the deep, thick silence held while Richard stared at me without expression until, with but the slightest quaver in his voice, he said quietly, "Sugar?"

It was ascertained that the painting had a thick leather band attached to the topside back of it that was looped over a roughly five inch long metal ingot driven into the wall at a steeply upward tilted angle. The ingot was still in place and the leather loop was still unbroken and attached to the painting. The dinner party broke up early.

Many years later, after he'd been stricken by multiple sclerosis, I tried to persuade Richard to reprise the role of Lionel Barrymore in a remake of that gloriously classic film, *On Borrowed Time*, but I couldn't get him to watch the original on a videocassette that I'd given him. "Tomorrow. No, not tomorrow. Tomorrow's Sunday, there's football," he'd say, or some such. The football excuse came on the Saturday that I picked him up from his wheelchair and set him down on his bed. Whatever it was that made me do it—the sheer innocence of the man, or just a genuine affection—as I was setting him down I lightly kissed him on the forehead, at which I thought I detected a slight lifting of his eyebrow in what could have been either surprise or an intense sudden wariness. It was the last time I'd ever see him. In this place.

INCIDENT #3

The time: between 1983 and 1985. The place: my former beach-house home, #29 in the Malibu Colony, where early one evening my wife Julie and I were sitting at the round, dark, oaken circular dining room table immediately adjacent to an open galley kitchen where on a section of its wall within about six or seven feet of us and facing a refrigerator on the opposite side hung a lightweight, yellow and white plastic battery-operated clock. Julie was seated facing the kitchen, while I sat with my back to it. First came loud rappings in a kitchen cabinet to our left. We started to talk about it, for the rappings were a persistent phenomenon that, for reasons I quite honestly cannot recall, weren't simply explicable by Karl the servant's line in *The Exorcist*, "maybe plumbing, maybe boards," when suddenly there came a loud crashing sound. I saw Julie's eyes flare wide open as she gasped, "My God, it just flew off the wall and crashed into the fridge!" "It" was the plastic clock. I got up and saw it lying on the floor half a foot from the bottom of the fridge. I then examined the nail on which the clock had been hanging. It was still firmly in place. Damien Karras, the priest in my novel, doubted every seemingly other-worldly occurrence with an obdurate intensity that was in fact in direct proportion to his yearning to believe. In this instance, my story was much the same. The next day, therefore, I replaced the nail from which the closed hook at the back of the clock had been hung with a thicker and longer nail which I hammered into place with an extreme upward tilt so that no seismic activity, no pounding of powerful waves against our wooden bulkheads, could possibly account for any future repeat of what had happened the night before. Yet it happened again. The next day? Days later? I would only be guessing. But this time as Julie and I sat at the dinner table, I was the one who was facing the kitchen when *bam! crash!* the plastic clock flew off the wall and banged into the bottom of the fridge with an explosive report. This time there was damage to the clock—a crack in its little glass window. I checked the nail. It was still intact and tilted radically upwards. Go figure.

INCIDENT #4

For this one I have a precise date, namely January 7, 1978, my birthday, when I was in Budapest, Hungary, directing the screenplay of my novel *The Ninth Configuration*. My cast included some of the most talented, intelligent, off-the-wall, and eccentric actors alive so that colorful events, shall we say, were not rare, one instance being Pulitzer Prize–winning dramatist Jason "Damien Karras" Miller and New York street-talking Joe Spinnell of the *Rocky* and *Godfather* movies awakening me by pounding on my door in the middle of the night to swear on their mothers' graves that a fight in the hotel disco involving full bottles of liquor from the bar's glass shelves being hurled at the Nigerian ambassador to Hungary and in which they were prime participants, was not their fault or, as Spinnell succinctly put it in describing the ambassador's triggering action, "The guy pulled a knife on us, Bill! Swear to God!!" My reaction to it all, as I recall, was a relative boredom inasmuch as just a week before, Nicol Williamson, perhaps the greatest movie Hamlet of all time and the actor I had originally cast in the lead role of "Killer" Kane, had not long before given me cause to feverishly recite the suicidally tinged "To be or not to be" soliloquy almost incessantly in both English and Arabic. I was so very fond of Nic! It was he who once told me a tale I still cherish, namely that while he was standing next to Noel Coward in a reception line of royals that ended with Queen Elizabeth, Chuck Connors, the very tall and ruggedly featured star of the popular TV series *The Rifleman*, thrust his enormous, beefy hand out to Coward as in a boomingly assertive voice he declared, "Mister Coward, I'm Chuck Connors!" at which the famed British playwright, while looking deep into Connors's eyes and after placing a comforting hand over both of their hands clasped together in a handshake, told Connors in that soothing, slightly strained, and overly reassuring tone of voice of someone who believes he is speaking to a madman, "Why, my dear boy of *course* you are!"

Williamson, normally incredibly fun and engaging, made his own contribution to wide-eyed incredulity as well, when on a night a few days prior to the start of principal photography and convincingly boxed, he kicked a room service waiter in his wisp of a fundament while calling him a "Communist bastard" out of total frustration at failing to make the hotel telephone operator understand that in order to reach Nicol's father in Scotland "one first has to go through a London exchange," as it was explained to me by Nicol the following morning in the calmly dispassionate British gentleman's hushed tone of voice that is used in the reading room of London clubs, a marked difference from his stance when, having kicked the operator, he then ripped the room telephone out of the wall, threw it through a window and onto the street four floors below, then a minute later appeared at the front desk of the Budapest Hilton to demand that the phone be reconnected. In fairness to Nic, God rest his soul, other than the desk clerk whom no one on the hotel staff liked or trusted, only one eyewitness to the event, a bellman whose understanding of English was minimal, was able to testify that Nic had then loudly added, "Wake up, you bloody aboriginals! Christ, we're living in the twentieth century in which telephones are actually expected to *work*!" Despite the thinness of the evidence, however, the Hungarian government declared Nicol *persona non grata* and I replaced him with Stacy Keach who gave a luminous performance. Out of evil comes good. At times.

Another likeable and quirky luminary among us was Neville Brand, the third most highly decorated American soldier in World War II. When asked when he was bitten by the show biz bug, Neville at first sighed, then stared off with a light of fond remembrance in his eyes as he recalled for us a time when he was with George Patton's Third Army and on the way to relieve beleaguered U.S. troops at Bastogne during the Battle of the Bulge. Patton's path was impeded by a German pillbox high on an embankment commanding the very narrow road. Early in the evening when it was thought that the Germans would be having dinner, Neville recounted, he was commissioned to single-handedly remove the impediment. "When I was almost where I was about to start sneaking up the hillside," he recalled, "I waited for a second to look behind me at the damn near endless line of American tanks and troops, and I thought, 'Holy Christ! They're all waiting on *me!*' and I think that's what did it. Yeah, that was it. That's when I caught the bug!" When Neville reached the pillbox undetected, he opened the door to find the Germans, as had been supposed, all at table eating dinner and in seconds he had sprayed them with bullets and killed them all. When someone among us asked, "Did you throw the door open, Neville?" he looked down and, slightly shaking his head, he said, "No. I pushed it open real slow." "What were you thinking at the time?" someone asked. Neville looked up into the questioner's eyes and said, "Nothing." A very quiet man, it was Jason Miller who once darkly observed of Brand, "I think Neville is lonely for his B.A.R." (Browning Automatic Rifle).

The most eyebrow-raising character amongst us was the Budapest Hilton Hotel itself. It had been built on the site of an ancient monastery, and before very long in the filming, two vivid and excited reports came from members of our British crew concerning sightings of ghosts in their rooms at night, the most vivid among them, perhaps, or at least the one that still has a firm grip on my memory, was by our young camera operator, Cary Fisher, the son of our cinematographer, the highly regarded Gerry Fisher who had also shot Nicol Williamson's *Hamlet*. A light sleeper, Cary awakened one night, he claimed, to find himself being stared at by, as he described it, "a very short monk-like hooded figure" standing silent and unmoving at the foot of his bed. Its face, Cary said, had a "Halloween pumpkin-like glow" and was pocked, little depressions emitting the strange faint orangish incandescence. Then came similar reports by others in the British crew, and it was Gerry Fisher who, researching the matter and getting his hands on the original plans of the monastery, discovered that the interior of the left-side wing of the hotel, in which all the British crew had their rooms, had been constructed within the still standing outer shell of the hotel's original monastery structure and this would explain, Fisher told me, why none of the Americans but only the British crew were reporting such sightings. He had also ascertained that the original third floor of the monastery—the floor now housing all the Brits—had actually been one foot lower than the present third floor. "Which explains," Gerry said without cracking a smile, "why the monks they keep seeing are all so bloody short."

Then came my fiftieth birthday, whose approach I celebrated by sitting at the hotel's disco bar with my production manager, Tom Shaw, who by midnight and the arrival of January 7 was soundly asleep, his head sagging down onto his chest. I shook him gently, saying, "Tom, say happy birthday." I heard a somnolent mumble. Tom's eyes were still closed. He hadn't lifted his head. "Say happy birthday," I repeated, and this time, with his eyes still closed, he complied. I went to my room, turned on the radio in time to hear a musical rendition of "Girl of My Dreams," a song I had always associated with my boyhood sweetheart, Mary nee McArdle of Woodside, New York. My eyebrows lifted. In Budapest, Hungary? I wondered wistfully, but only for a moment, if it could possibly be Mary wishing me a Happy 50th Birthday. I went to bed and had a dreamless sleep.

The next morning I checked the front desk for messages. There was one, a telegram on yellowish paper. Its message:

HAPPY BIRTHDAY, DEAR BILL
YOUR BROTHER, RAY

I did indeed have a brother named Raymond. He had died in infancy.

Not wishing to withhold any possibly explanatory detail from you, I should also report that I telephoned my brother in San Diego that day and asked if he had sent me a birthday telegram. He said that he had.

"Didn't you get it?" he asked.

"Yes, I got it. Eddie, how did you sign it?"

"What?"

"How did you sign it?"

"'Your brother Eddie.'"

"You didn't sign it 'Ray'?"

"Sign it what?"

"Never mind."

Though I don't know what to make of it, that isn't quite all. According to my sister Alice, for two or three years after Raymond's passing, my mother prayed fervently and relentlessly every single day that God would send him back to her. And then along came Bill. When I was living in Connecticut, I learned for the first time from Father William Wood, my former Jesuit teacher at The Prep, that January 7, the date of my birth, is the Feast of Saint Raymond.

INCIDENT #5

At age nine, my brilliant and wonderful grandson Bradley contracted what at first was diagnosed as "cat scratch fever," but then later was discovered to be a very rapid-spreading cancer. With family gathered in a hospital lounge while surgeons operated on Brad, after about three hours a surgeon informed us that the cancerous mass still growing inside him was found to be so thick that it was pointless to attempt removal. "Are you saying that only a miracle can save him?" asked my son Michael. The surgeon hesitated a moment, then nodded and said gravely, "Yes." He gave Bradley six weeks to live.

At the time I was busy with preproduction for *The Ninth Configuration*, and riding along the Pacific Coast Highway with Tom Shaw, I was thinking of a surprisingly favorable article I had read in *Time* magazine about a faith healer named Kathryn Kuhlman. I'd been telling Shaw about Brad and at one point blurted out, "God, I wish I knew someone who could get me to Kathryn Kuhlman!" I was instantly informed that such a person was Shaw. "Yeah, I'm friends with Tom Lewis, Loretta Young's ex-husband and Loretta and this Kuhlman, they're real tight, they're very close friends." Shaw said he'd call Lewis and before very long I was directly in touch with Kathryn Kuhlman. I had thrown on a jacket and was about to leave my Santa Monica beach-house and drive to visit Bradley at the L.A. Children's Hospital when the telephone rang. I glanced at my watch. I was running a bit late. Should I answer? I picked up the phone, said "Hello" and the next thing I heard was, "Mr. Blatty, this is Kathryn Kuhlman. I am about to go out on stage here in Dallas where some six thousand people will be praying for your grandson." I remember nothing else of the conversation other than her repeating more than once, "Watch for a change."

Arriving at the hospital, I was redirected from Brad's room to another where I found him on an examination table with his mother, my daughter Christine, standing by him. Now hear this, if you would. Really listen. Prior to this moment, Brad had for over a week been running a temperature, had been unremittingly sullen and non-communicative, had no appetite, and now was scheduled for surgery the next day to remove cancerous tissue obstructing a bowel-cleaning catheter. But then came "a change." First, barely a minute after my arrival, my daughter's eyebrows lifted in glad surprise as she pointed at the catheter measurement markings and breathed out in glad surprise, "Oh, my gosh, Dad, look! The catheter's gone down all on its own!" Then I was told that as of that morning, Bradley's temperature had dropped to normal, he'd said he was hungry, and I could see for myself that his eyes were clear as he avidly talked his head off about a little boy's ordinary topics of interest. The following day's surgery was canceled, then later in the day I was informed of a far more major "change." In daily X-rays, an ominous mass in Brad's chest had been seen to be growing steadily larger and larger; but that afternoon, my daughter told me that night, when the daily X-ray was taken the result caused the lab technician to turn to her and tell her with a quiet and subdued astonishment, "There seems to be some kind of exorcism going on here." The lethal mass had entirely vanished and at the end of the fated six weeks my grandson wasn't dead, he was back in school. I so wish I could end the report of this incident right there, but so that you have all the facts in making whatever judgment you are going to make, I am bound to report that some year and a half later, while cautious and perhaps disbelieving medics continued giving Bradley cobalt radiation treatment, he was attacked by the same rapid-spreading cancer. This time no "exorcism" intervened. I should also report, I suppose, that a day or two after Brad's passing, his mother's television set, which she tells me was not turned on at the time, suddenly exploded with its glass screen shattering into shards.

Brad.

INCIDENT #6

In 1961 I read a fascinating book by Bishop James Pike called *The Other Side* in which Pike recounted what he believed were "messages" from Jim, his son, who had taken his own life at the age of twenty. Along the way Pike mentioned going to an alleged psychic in Santa Barbara named Reverend George Daisley, whom he finally judged to be the "real thing," although Pike qualified his assessment because psychics reputedly cannot press a button and find themselves communicating with the dead "on demand," and in moments when their powers fail and they are paid for their services "they vamp." Still deeply—perhaps even neurotically—grieving over Mama's death, I determined to meet with Daisley, and on the appointed day I drove from Woodland Hills, California, to Santa Barbara, along with a friend of those days named Beth. Once there, the Reverend Daisley provided each of us with a blue-lined yellow pad and pencil on which we were told to make notes of his statements, after which, in a room brightly lit by late morning sunshine streaming through tall, wide windows, Daisley seated himself opposite us in a straight-backed wooden chair, lowered his head, clasped his hands across his stomach, and began transmitting "messages from the beyond," during which he exemplified Pike's observation that he sometimes "vamped," for while making a few strong "hits" he also had some misses, one of which was actually rather comical. He had "psychically" asserted that I had two children, and when I shook my head and said, "No, I have five," Daisley vigorously slapped his upper thigh with a hand and rasped "*Damn!*" But then along came something else. Just a week or two before, Beth was telling me about her "Granny Dot" and her beloved pet bird—either a parrot or a parakeet, I can't recall which. Beth had lifted her head, wistfully staring off as she said, "I wonder where that bird is now" and then wondered aloud whether or not there was an afterlife for animals. And now, in the midst of this brightly lit séance, out of nowhere, George Daisley, attributing the "message" to an unnamed female relative of Beth's, said, "*Tell her the bird is over here with us.*"

INCIDENT #7

Remember my telling you how when Mama and I were out quincing the wind blew a dollar bill into my chest? As usual, I can't remember the date but it was not long after publication of *The Exorcist* that, while walking on 57th Street with an actress friend named Kathy Gerber on a breezy evening early in November, I had just finished telling her the story of the wind-driven dollar bill when *a wind blew another one straight into my chest!* Yes! I don't know what it means, but it happened! As we crossed the street on Madison Avenue, standing at the corner was a slender, dark-skinned woman in her sixties wearing gypsy attire. She was staring at me sharply, eyes gleaming. I thought of Mama and gave her a twenty.

INCIDENT #8

In 1968 I determined once and for all that I would write the novel about demonic possession, and to that end, bringing with me two pages of typed notes (see Exhibit "B" on page 207) containing all that I knew about what I was to write, I rented a spare little cabin in the hills above Lake Tahoe where over the course of some six weeks I succeeded in emulating the Jack Nicholson role in Stephen King's terrifying *The Shining* as over and over again I kept repeating the same paragraph beginning, "The mysterious rappings began on the night of April 1." I would read the paragraph aloud, find the rhythm ungainly and, day after day, week after week, would change the date from April whatever to April something else, a phenomenon that I at first attributed to my having no plot but that one day long after I would diagnose as my unconscious mind telling me I was starting the novel in the wrong place, which was Georgetown, when I ought to be starting in Northern Iraq. But at the time I lacked that insight and after a week or two of this insanity and growling "I can't take this pressure anymore!" I sauntered down to the Cal Neva Casino where I spent most of the hours of my day at the blackjack tables and where, after

I had won the enormous sum of $600 one day, the casino manager spread the word to the dealers, most of them young women, that I was a professional gambler and that they should use not a single deck but two whenever I played at their table, a situation blossoming into near hilarity when one of the dealers decided I wasn't a card shark but in fact was the former New York Jets quarterback, Joe Namath. I don't think the casino manager believed her because he sicced a "cooler" on me, a very elderly man who sat at my table with the intent of breaking my winning streak, and who after being dealt his first two cards took nearly a full minute to stare at his bottom card before turning it over to reveal he had a blackjack. It was maddening. And it worked. I started losing heavily, quit the tables in a funk, and went downstairs to the casino's health room facility where, just before entering a sauna, having learned from experience that because it was metal the heat of the sauna would eventually cause it to burn my skin, I removed Mama's medal and placed it on a table and then afterwards, after exiting the sauna, I of course put it on again, went home, tried to work, couldn't, and went to bed. It's about what happened the next morning after I'd awakened. As I bent my head low over the bathroom sink while brushing my teeth, I heard an odd clinking sound, straightened up, looked in the mirror and saw hanging from my neck not just Mama's medal but also a second one. Small and round and bearing a likeness of the Blessed Virgin Mary, it was of a coppery color that was largely covered over by a greenish mold, suggesting that the wearer very rarely, or more likely never, removed it when showering or bathing. It was also, to the best of my recollection at that time, identical to the second medal that Mama was wearing and that I'd left in place when she died.

In the days to come I made several calls to the manager of the spa to ask whether anyone had called or come by asking about a lost or missing holy medal. No one had. When I finally explained to the sauna manager why I'd been asking, he had a facile explanation. "You come out of the sauna, you are groggy, you pick up the wrong medal." I leave it to you to judge his explanation. Sometime after that I told my brother Moe what had happened and showed him the medal. "Isn't this exactly like the one Mama wore?" I asked him. Staring down at it fixedly, Moe nodded his head a little, then said quietly, "Yes." He then asked if he could keep it.

INCIDENT #9

Early in 1972, Dr. Thelma Moss, a psychology professor, headed UCLA's Neuropsychiatric Institute, which had a laboratory dedicated to research in parapsychology. As part of his research into paranormal phenomena before directing *The Exorcist*, Billy Friedkin thought we should pay it a visit. Moss had lined up a young police officer whom she said was a psychometrist, someone into whose hand you could place an object from which he could "read things" about you or some event in your life. She asked me to give her something I'd had for a very long time and I gave her Mama's medal, the silvery one that I had kept and worn without ever removing it up to that point for almost five years. She then called the young policeman into the room. He sat down in a chair, Moss gave him my mother's medal without telling him whether it had come from me or Billy Friedkin, and for a time he closed his eyes and kept it gripped in his fist. Then he spoke. "It's very strange," he said; "one half of it [the medal] is warm and the other half is cold." Why, yes, I reflected in wonder: it had belonged to someone dead and has been worn now for years by someone who is alive! The young policeman then went on to tell us that he "saw" a white wooden house with a white wooden fence around it. It was close to a railroad yard, he said, and by the house there was a black and white spotted dog. To me, none of that meant a thing. No. Not then. But sometime later—maybe months, maybe even a year—I asked my sister Alice whether or not, when she was living in Lebanon with my mother and father and brothers, did they ever live in a white frame house with a white picket fence, and Alice answered, "Yes." And had a black and white spotted dog?

Again, a "yes." And anywhere close to a railroad yard? "Oh, well, yes," she answered. "Papa worked for the railroad. Why, Willie?" I wasn't crazy enough to tell her.

INCIDENT #10

London, the early 1960s. I'm in the Dorchester Hotel writing the first draft of the Peter Sellers Inspector Clouseau movie, *A Shot in the Dark*, and how I got to this point might be worth a mention. It began at the Goldwyn Studios in Hollywood where I was writing the screenplay of *What Did You Do in the War, Daddy?* for director Blake Edwards. In fact, and I mention it only in passing, this was the very same day that at a breakfast table in the Goldwyn lot cafeteria that I asked Billy Wilder by what genius he was able to put all of those wonderful "director's touches" into his films and in reply he had uttered those immortal words, "What touches? I *put it in the script!*" Then at lunch Blake gave me the news that the director filming a version of *A Shot in the Dark* that adhered closely to the more or less straight play by Marcel Achard had left the picture and that Blake had been offered the job. "I won't do it unless you write it," he told me. I spent the rest of the day and most of that night and next morning reading the play and trying to assess whether I was the person to do it justice, and at the end of it all a new direction to the story occurred to me that I quickly typed up in a page and a half that proposed the following plot: dead body after dead body is found consecutively murdered in the mansion of a French millionaire. Obviously, each successive murder is aimed at covering up those previous to it, right? Right? Well, wrong. Each is committed, I proposed, by a different murderer for a totally different motive. But the plot could only work for me, I insisted, if Peter Sellers were to reprise his role of the bumbling Inspector Clouseau in director Edwards's uproarious *The Pink Panther*. Blake shook his head. "He'll never do it," he said. But Sellers agreed. And now we are back at "The

Dorch" in London. It's late morning and I'm working in a central "office" space with a door to Blake's suite to my right and Sellers's—I believe it was labeled "The Oliver Messel Suite"—to my left. I was typing away and dreaming of having scones with jam and Chantilly Cream with my lunch when a loud banging sound drew my gaze to my left and a heavily draped windowed wall looking out to the street three floors below. On the floor I saw a very large plant with a shattered clay pot that had fallen off its pedestal. Odd. I stood up and walked over to investigate. The pot had a flat, square base that measured about a foot and a half by a foot and a half and the top of the very large and heavy pedestal it had fallen from was square and as flat as the base of the fallen pot. Had a sudden wind or breeze somehow unsettled it? As heavy drapes had been drawn across all of the windows behind the potted plant, that possibility seemed a bit doubtful, but I pulled aside the drapes to discover that no eerie winds were in evidence and that anyway all the windows were closed. There had been a previous occasion when I had asked Sellers why he'd sold the home that he several times told us he loved, eliciting this interesting answer: "Well, when I was sitting on the edge of my bed after waking up one morning and saw both my socks levitate up to the level of my eyes, I decided I'd had enough of all the knockings and rappings and footsteps in the middle of the night in an empty house." And so it was mostly as a bit of a jest, and partly pay-back for his having called down to my room and awakening me from sleep at around half past three one morning to ask me to repeat a joke I had told him earlier in the day—Peter clearly had company—that led me to knock on the door to his suite and then lead him to the site of the shattered planter. Putting on a look of grave concern, "See what your poltergeist has just done?" I said in an accusatory tone, at which Sellers, looking down at the mess on the floor, said softly and apologetically, "Oh, Bill, I'm so terribly sorry" and then wordlessly padded back to his suite. And lest you think Peter Sellers was a credulous, starry-eyed mystic, I offer you this portion of a letter that he wrote to me years later:

PETER SELLERS

Via Appia Antica 201,
Rome.

28th November, 1966

W. P. Blatty, Esq.,
4630 Balboa Boulevard,
ENCINO, Calif.

Dear Bill,

Your letter and script arrived, and the outline looks very promising. It will obviously need
careful development so as not to fall into the Carry
On Holmes category. I mean merely to point out
that this can be one of the dangers - Derek Dangers
....you remember....used to be a friend of the
Worthington-Smythes,...but then, how can one ever
forget Piggy Worthington-Smythe....One of their
pigs, ectualleh.

And with that joyous message ringing in our
ears, we say farewell to colourful Baker Street with
the words of G. K. Betjamanajee, er.... ringing in
our ears

The stingy Maharajah of Baroda
Would not pay a whore what he owed her.
She said, "That's not fair!",
As she stood on his chair
And pissed in his whiskey and soda.

love,

[signature]

INCIDENT #11

My wife Julie was the witness to this and so I will let her tell it in her own words: "When our son Paul was about eighteen months old, we were living in a rented ocean-side home in Santa Barbara, California. Because the house was rented, Paul's room was furnished with only the necessities: his crib, a changing table, a rocking chair, and a small bookcase with toys and books. One night, as I was nursing Paul to sleep in the rocking chair, he startled me by suddenly sitting bolt upright in my lap, thrusting his arm out stiffly and pointing to the dark and empty corner of the room across from the chair. I was startled in part because Paul was an avid nursling, and pretty much nothing could get him to break suction. I was doubly startled by the beatific look on his little face. His eyes were locked onto some ineffable sight that only he could see as he pointed straight into the empty corner of the room with his pudgy little finger. 'Ghosht,' he breathed out. Intrigued, I asked him if the ghost was a man. He simply shook his head, no. Next I asked if the ghost was a woman. Another shake of his head. 'Well,' I asked finally, 'then what kind of ghost was it?' and he broke into a glorious smile and simply said, 'Happy.' After that, he resumed his nursing as if nothing out of the ordinary had happened, and promptly fell sound asleep. I like to think it was his Guardian Angel."

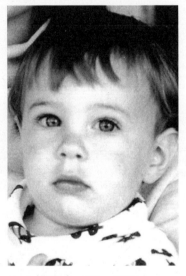

Paulie: "Ghosht!!"

Sadly, the experience left Paulie scarred. Witness his matching outfit on the first day he was ever allowed to dress himself.

INCIDENT #12

In the autumn of 1974 I spent a couple of months in Jerusalem researching a planned theological thriller to be entitled *Dimiter* in which the protagonist would parallel certain episodes in the life of Christ, some of them explanatory; for instance, it would suggest that Christ had to die horrifically by public crucifixion not to satisfy a bloodlust for "settling accounts" by the Father, but rather because had He died in bed of pneumonia we would never have heard of Him, resurrected or not.* I returned home to Los Angeles laden with tapes, notes, and a manuscript about the tracking down and capture of the Nazi war criminal Adolf Eichmann written and given to me to help me in my research by Isser Harel, who had masterminded the hunt and came to be known as the "father of Israeli intelligence." An avuncular dumpling of a man, Harel told me that his manuscript called *The House on Garibaldi Street* had never been published because when he'd submitted it to authorities for clearance some of the operatives named in the book were still alive. "And are they now?" I'd asked Harel at our meeting in my room at the King David Hotel. "No, all are now dead," he'd replied. "So why not publish now?" I asked, and he looked away with a distant despondency and a gentle shaking of his head as he quietly answered, "No, now nobody cares." As it happened, however, once home, and without Harel's knowledge, I called my Bantam editor and *Exorcist* savior Marc Jaffe about it, and was able one day to surprise Isser Harel by calling him in Israel to tell him that Bantam Books wanted to publish his book that nobody cared about with an advance of one hundred thousand dollars, at which the first response at Harel's end of the call was a gasping intake of breath, and then a little spate of stunned and unbelieving sputtering which lasted through Harel's stammering, excited exclamation, "Mr. Blatty, *I like you very much!*" And so good: I had solved Harel's publishing problem. But would you believe that over the next thirty-six years I was able to produce no more than one hundred six pages of *my* book? Oh, I'd tried. My *God*, how I'd tried! Unlike with *The Exorcist*, this time I had all my characters and a fully

---

* Three years ago, *The Exorcist* director Billy Friedkin who, like his wife the former Sherri Lansing, is Jewish, told me that he and Sherri abruptly stood up and left a Hollywood party in disgust upon hearing one of the guests asserting there was no evidence of any kind that the person called Jesus Christ ever existed.

outlined, very detailed plot, but not only was the latter devilishly compli-
cated, but because it would have ruined the explosive surprise at the end,
I wasn't ever permitted to get into the protagonist's head. Hard cheese. So
I put the book aside, and wrote some others. But then conscience—yes,
conscience—at last brought me back to it. You see, from the start I had
conceived of *Dimiter* as an apostolic work, and in 1996 when I was stricken
by cancer, I had promised God that if I lived through it I would put aside
everything and complete it. Being a flaky writer, I welshed, that's what
writers do; but years later, prodded by the sting of guilt, I once again took
up the novel in the late 1990s for yet another hopeless stab at success,
going back and forth over and over again about what elements the following chapter—Chapter Six—should contain until finally, exhausted and
defeated, I finally, decisively gave up.

Then something happened. In the spring of 2008 my wife Julie and
I attended a memorial mass for Tommy Carroll, one of my son Peter's
classmates at The Heights in Potomac, Maryland, and while at times
during Sunday sermons my mind tends to wander a bit, on this particular occasion the priest's homily had a very firm grip on my attention when suddenly, and without a word in the sermon that might have
triggered it, the single word "Dimiter" struck at my consciousness like
a branding iron slammed against my forehead. Like a voiceless shout.
I cannot properly describe it, other than to say that while I really didn't
see or hear a thing, whatever had happened was so clearly and strongly
out of the ordinary that I actually responded to the source of it, which,
being Catholic, I reflexively identified as the Holy Spirit, and so it came
to be that with a certain irritation and abrasiveness I mentally flung
back, like a challenge, "Oh, well, fine! You really want me that badly to
finish it? Well, then, show me how to do it, would you please? Just *show*
me!"

About twenty minutes later as Julie and I were exiting the chapel, I put
an arm across Julie's path to prevent her from proceeding toward our car
in The Heights School parking lot as with a rushed but quiet excitement I

proceeded to tell her how in a single panoramic flash of—what? I didn't know—I saw precisely how to structure and finish the novel. "I even know the last line!" I declared: "'Meral smiled.'" The next morning, after Julie had left for Chicago to visit family, I went to work and eighteen days and nights later completed a draft of the novel that to this day I believe to be the most important I have ever written. And, yes: the last line is "Meral smiled."

And so what was it that had happened here? Had the Holy Spirit actually infused the content of my novel into my mind before the mass had ended? The psychiatrist Carl Jung once asserted that the unconscious mind was probably fifty times more knowledgeable and intelligent than the one we walk around with all our waking days and I can confidently assure you that psychologists the world over and in ever colorful and flowering abundance will explain that my ability to so suddenly and quickly complete the novel was merely yet one more instance of the mysterious, if not unfathomable, workings of the unconscious mind. And they could be right. Or not.

INCIDENT #13: DREAMS OF THE FUTURE

In the thirty-five years since my boyhood triumph in The Strange Case of 059, I either didn't have, or was simply unaware of having, anything that one could at least suspect was a precognitive dream. Not one. But then I read a book called *An Experiment with Time* that was given to me by Ellen Burstyn. Originally published in 1927, it was written by the British mathematician and aeronautical engineer J. W. Dunne. He had dreamed he was standing in the middle of a road on a volcanic island shouting at the passengers of oncoming carriages, "Get off the island! 40,000 are going to die!" Three days later while sitting in his club, he came upon an article in *The Times of London* reporting that 4,000 people had been killed the day before in a volcanic eruption on an island. And then a few days after that, the *Times* lowered its report of the number killed to

3,700. More and more of Dunne's dreams followed this pattern, from which he concluded that these pre-cognitive dreams were not the product of some psychic ability, but rather, as with his dream of the volcanic island, a pre-view of an actual event roughly three days later, in this case reading in his club the erroneous report of 4,000 killed, which in his dream was 40,000, when in fact a truly psychic event would have forecast the actual death toll of 3,700. Dunne replicated his experience in experiments with thousands of students at his university, resulting in his conclusion that everyone, in fact, dreams the future. The trick was to notice it. So I followed the mathematician's advice that on awakening each day one should immediately write down what one remembers from one's dreams and that usually a few days later, though it might be as long as several months, their notes would be corroborated by events. Here below are the few of these dreams that I remember.

1) I dream I see floating in mid-air in the beach-house room in which I am sleeping an open casket containing the body of an olive-skinned girl. She is resting on her back and bears some resemblance to me. When I awaken I am worried about my twenty-two-year-old daughter Christine. Six weeks later my sister Alice, healthy and aged fifty-six, unexpectedly dies in her sleep.

2) A much better dream. I am living in the Encino guest house in which I was writing my novel *The Exorcist.* I have a little money saved from my screenwriting gigs and it is all invested in corporate bonds whose prices had been recently battered. Then I dream I am in a hotel lobby and am walking to the front desk arm in arm with Hal Lehrman, who had given my first novel a wonderful review in the *New York Herald Tribune.* When we get to the desk, my eye runs along the top row of message boxes until it halts midway between Box 140 and Box 150. I ask the desk clerk, "Anything in 130?" At this point I have read Dunne's book and suspect I've had one of those "future dreams." I sat at my desk and searched through that day's Wall Street listings for any corporate bond at a price of 130. There was only one—Allegheny Ludlum. Then on a sheet of paper

I wrote "Hal Lehrman" in block letters, and beneath it the name of the bond.

HALLEHRMAN

ALLEGHENYLUDLUM

By ignoring the initial "H," I saw the match between the first four letters on each line and, yes, being halfway crazy, I called my stock broker and told him to buy Allegheny Ludlum at a price of 130. Minutes or so later he called me to say that the bond had suddenly jumped to a price of 132. "Still want it?" he asked. I said no. I wasn't *that* crazy. But then later the broker called again to say the bond's price had dropped back to 130 and did I still want it. I said yes, and within about a week or ten days the price of Allegheny Ludlum had risen to somewhere in the low one hundred forties and, remembering the box number at which my vision in the dream halted, the next day I told the broker to sell it. The following day the price of the bond began a precipitate slide that soon ended in the low 120s.

3) Another stock market dream. I cannot remember the name of my holding except that it was a "blue chip." When it's price was $18—the number is vividly recalled—I dreamed that I was looking at a price quote for the stock through a large, round magnifying glass and that it had dropped to 1 3/4. My thoughts were that a drop in price that steep for a blue chip stock was so wildly improbable that the dream couldn't possibly be precognitive dreaming. Sometime later, and for reasons that had nothing to do with the dream, I sold the stock. A couple of months later I found that its price had dropped to 1 3/4. Ah! It just came to me. The stock was Sony.

4) I dream I'm in a tennis doubles match the night before such a match has been scheduled. My partner is Linda nee Tuero, many times amateur national champion, ranked as high as #7 in pro women's world rankings and once winner of the Italian Open. The dream is brief, just a snapshot

in which I am rushing to save Linda from one of our opponents, a man wearing a doctor's medical whites who has a dagger in his upraised hand and is about to stab her in the heart. The next day Ms. Tuero and I are in fact playing doubles against two married friends, Marcos and Linda Fleiderman. We are closing out a game. Linda uncorks a terrific serve to Marcos, who mis-hits it, catching it off the edge of his racket. The ball sails lazily, hits the top of the net, and spins there for a bit as I'm desperately rushing forward but fail to reach it before its second bounce. We lose point and game and as we switch to the opposite side of the court, I put my arm around Tuero's shoulder, saying guardedly, "How about that flukey return by Marcos!" to which she answered, "Oh, God, it was like a knife in my heart." Instantly I remembered the dream. And the fact that Marcos was an M.D.

5) Mid-1980s. We are living in Greenwich, Connecticut. It's early morning. Julie and I will soon be leaving for Manhattan to meet with a realtor and look at a possible pied-à-terre in Greenwich Village and are breakfasting when Julie tells me she had dreamed that we were living in Manhattan and that while standing on a balcony she looked down and to her right and saw the movie star Kathleen Turner putting out her garbage on the sidewalk. "Oh, does she live in the Village?" I asked and Julie answered either no or that she had no idea. Then in town, and while inspecting the Greenwich Village fourth floor apartment, I expressed an apprehensiveness about security in what I believed was a crime-ridden area, to which one of the owners of the property scoffed, "Oh, come on! There's no security problem here! I mean, Kathleen Turner lives right next door!" He was gesturing to the right.

6) Another Julie experience and one that I don't quite know how to categorize other than as "a waking dream." Here's Julie: "I'll never forget the date, January 27, 1986, which I remember because the next day was my father's birthday, and as my parents were visiting us in Connecticut I was looking forward to celebrating with him. Bill and I were on our way to the local Grand Union grocery store to pick up a few items for the next day.

Bill was driving and I remember sitting in the front passenger seat, lost in thought. Suddenly, an image flooded my mind's eye and I saw with great clarity the front page of a newspaper. Above the fold were featured head shots of all the Shuttle astronauts, smiling innocently, and I knew instantly, heartbreakingly, that they had all died. The next day, January 28, the space shuttle *Challenger* exploded in mid-air shortly after takeoff, killing all aboard."

7) And of course, there is the matter of 059, a precise and specific dream of the immediate future about which there is an additional story to tell. You recall that the man in my dream who looked down at me and said, "Play 059" had an aquiline and slightly hooked nose and was wearing a dark fedora with a colorful feather in its band? Well, in later years while I was in the fifth grade at St. Stephen's Parochial School on East 28th Street in Manhattan, for a while we lived in an apartment on East 35th Street around the corner from a cigarette, newspaper, candy, and magazine shop called "Boshnack's" where while loitering and passing the time I would often watch a man in his early twenties playing the shop's lone pinball machine, and who was uncannily skillful at shaking the machine into doing his bidding without it ever registering "*Tilt*." I can't remember his name, but—and of this I am quite positive—he was the very image, including the fedora and the feather in its band, of the man who said "Play 059" in my boyhood dream. I've had other such dreams. Many. And if J. W. Dunne was correct so have you. He concluded such dreams were proof of the existence of the soul.

INCIDENT #14

Maybe 1968. It is night and while discussing a screenplay I have been contracted to write for Paul Newman, I am sitting with him in his Beverly Hills Hotel bungalow drinking gin and tonics out of a pair of his shoes because the hotel housekeeping unit has neglected to provide the bungalow with drinking glasses, which, considering the hotel's reputation, the cost of one of its bungalows, and the fact that its occupant was a superstar, I am scrapping my phony stance of objectivity and declaring it a definite paranormal event.

And so now here we are at a moment of decision. The question is not whether you believe that the incidents recounted above are in fact paranormal phenomena; rather, it is whether or not you trust me to have told you the absolute and total truth of them. If your answer is anywhere in the area of "Not on your life!" the most kindly advice I can give you is not to go on to what follows. It would be wasting your time. There isn't the slightest chance you would believe it.

PART FOUR

Proof of Life

So many people imagine that death cruelly separates us from our loved ones. Even pious people are led to believe this great and sad mistake. Death is not a separation. When our loved one dies, they do not leave us. They remain. They do not go to some distant place. They simply begin their eternity. Death has not destroyed them, nor carried them away. Rather it has given them life and the power to know and love us more fully than ever before. The tears that dampen our eyes in times of mourning are tears of homesickness, tears of longing for our loved ones. But it is we who are far from home, not they. Death has been for them a doorway to eternal home. And only because this home is invisible to our worldly eyes, we cannot see them so near us, lovingly and tenderly waiting for the day when we, too, will enter the doorway. And then we will see them.

—Cardinal John Henry Newman

Blessed are they who mourn, for they will laugh.

—Luke 6:21

THIRTEEN

My son Peter was mystery enough in himself. When he was but a month old, I entered his room in the Greenwich, Connecticut, home in which Julie and I were then living, rested my arms on the top of one of the sides of his crib and looked down at him. He was lying on his back, his eyes open. I saw his lips move and I heard him say clearly, "I love you," and then instantly, reflexively, I answered without thinking, "I love you, too." The next voice I heard was Julie's. She had been entering the room and now came up beside me. "Oh, you heard it, too!" she said. "I thought I was imagining it!" As the years slid by, Peter's mystery only grew. Julie kept a contemporaneous diary of statements he had made from earliest childhood that were—well— unusual. At the age of three, for instance, while Julie was changing our younger son Paul in our new Santa Barbara home, Peter was standing at a refectory window staring out at the freshness of day when he said, without turning and in a faraway voice, "Do you know why I came here, Mommy?" Julie said, "No, Petey, why?" and he answered, "I came here to help people." At age three. Think about it. Not "I was born" but "I *came* here!" At the same age, he once confronted me to ask, "Daddy, how do you learn?" I said, "Through reading and experience," and he shook his head and said, "That's not how *I* learn. I learn from the sky. God teaches me." And when he was five and we were living in Hidden Hills, California, one day Peter approached his mother and said, "You know, Mom, when God was making me, I was a little bit sad and a little bit scared. But then I saw you." It's in the diary. Word for word.

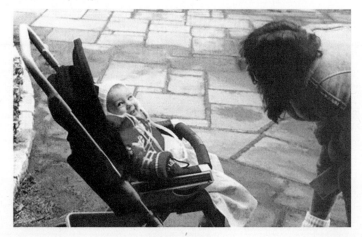

Here I come!

1990: "Ghosht" time in Santa Barbara.

Greenwich, Connecticut, 1988.

Thanksgiving Day, 1988.
Always ready to give.

"I came here to help people."

"But then I saw YOU."

Regarding Peter's spirituality, Julie's diary reveals quite an interesting range. When he was six he told his mother that while he believed everything written in the Bible, he then added, and I quote, "But I just can't get behind a talking snake!" Then jump ahead to a diary entry made in his final year of his earthly life: "Oh, Mom…if I had lived in the time of Christ and had been able to see Him and hear Him, I just know I couldn't have resisted Him!" Are you getting a picture of some ascetic and droop-eyed mystic? Forget it!

Here he is at age seventeen.

"A larger than life personality."

It was the rare individual who, on first meeting Pete, that imposing young man with a quick, warm smile, didn't sense that he was somehow in the presence of an extraordinary human being. In his high school yearbook he was described as "a larger than life personality." There were never any halfway measures with Peter. Fiercely loyal and fiercely faithful, his love burned brightly and intensely like the love of angels massed before God. For many years he thought everyone was built that way, and so it was easy to break his heart. But like his scriptural namesake, Pete would have cut off the High Priest's servant's ear without a moment of hesitation. He was incredibly brave. And kind. I couldn't drive past a beggar on a median strip without Peter pleading that I give the man money. "We'll hold up traffic, son. Can't do it." "Come on Dad, *please!*" A week or two after Peter had left this vale of tears, a young man named Noah Hopkins, a former Heights classmate of Peter's, came by with a very young dogwood tree. He wanted to plant it in our yard in his memory. And "In gratitude," he said. He then told me a story of when he and Peter were both fifteen. The friend had challenged a boy from another school to a fight. They met in a field, surrounded by about eighty boys from both schools. They fought and Noah won the bout. But the vanquished boy threatened he'd fetch a cousin who would then beat Noah to a pulp, to which Noah responded, "Fine. Bring him on. Bring an army." What showed up was almost worse: a hulking, muscular twenty-six-year-old ex-convict who had just been released from prison. Within minutes, Noah was on the ground, taking blow after blow to the face and head, and recognizing that he was in danger of serious injury he shouted, "Stop! Stop! I give up!" But the man didn't stop. Among those eighty watching the fight were several hulking football players. But they didn't intervene. No one moved. Except Peter. He slipped out of the crowd, walked up to the convict, who was flailing away at Noah, and said commandingly, "Didn't you hear him say stop? He said stop! So now do it!" And in an almost mysterious, otherworldly moment, the hulking ex-con looked up at Peter with a numb and bewildered look on his face and then got up without a word and walked away. On the day he brought the

tree to our house for planting, Noah said he'd chosen a species of dogwood
called, "Cherokee Brave." Youthful idealism sometimes prompts a boy to
utter, "Oh, I'd give up my life for him or her." What made Peter unique
was that if he ever said such a thing you knew that he would actually do it.
"I came here to help people." Yes. In great things and in small. And even
in the midst of affliction. Near the end of his life, Peter was gripped in the
remorseless coils of bipolar disorder type one, even slashing his wrists one
nightmarish day. And what did Julie and I find him doing when we came
to visit him in the hospital? He was teaching a young girl how to say the
rosary.

   And then along came that autumn-spackled, crisp sunny day near the
end of orange October of 2006 when, while driving on a wooded street
close to my home, out of nowhere I found myself thinking about my age
and that I'd had such an easy life for so long, when I died how could I possibly squeeze through that scriptural "narrow gate" into heaven? "I've got
seven children," my thoughts continued, "and not one of them has died."
I would swear to the truth of this on my deathbed. And, as you will see, in
view of what happened next, how could I possibly ever forget it? A week or
so later, Peter had a perfectly wonderful day: his boxing coach had called
to assure him that though he had warned Peter he would no longer coach
him if ever Pete was found to have taken drugs, nevertheless he was giving
him another chance; then I authorized a ludicrously generous amount of
money for Pete to be able to bid for speedy possession of some new Xbox;
and later he was having friends over for pizza and beer and to watch the
Raiders, Petey's favorite pro football team, play in the first of their games
ever to be televised in the area since we had moved to Maryland. Around
8 p.m. I ran into Pete and he hugged me and said, "Goodnight, Dad," to
which I replied, "Why goodnight already? I'll be around." Yet that night I
never saw him again.

   Julie did. She went down into the basement den to bid him goodnight.
As she re-ascended the stairs, he called two things out to her. The first was,
"Mom, they said in rehab that once you're a pickle, you can't turn back into

a cucumber again. But I showed 'em, didn't I, Mom? Do I get props for that?" The other was a statement that has haunted me mysteriously and warmly to this day and for reasons I prefer not to discuss, other than to say that when I saw the bones of St. Peter in the underground tunnels of the Scavi in Rome many years ago, I fell to my knees and kept murmuring over and over, "I love you. I love you. I love you," for he'd been my favorite saint ever since reading in the gospels how at the sight of the resurrected Christ standing on the shore, while the other apostles excitedly rowed toward him, his disciple Peter was so in love with Christ that he threw on a cloak, leaped overboard and began to swim furiously toward him. The second—and last—thing that Petey had called up to his mother was, "Mom, I'm so lucky Paul loves me!"

Around half past six the next morning, November 7, Julie awakened with a feeling that something was somehow amiss. She got up out of bed, checked Peter's room, and not finding him there, she went down to our basement den where Peter and his friends had watched the Raiders game. The friends had long since left, but the TV was still on and Peter, his eyes open, the TV remote still cradled in a hand and a pleasant expression on his face, was sitting up on the sofa as if still watching it. Except that he wasn't. Emptied of breath by viral myocarditis, an extremely rare disorder that gives little or no warning before the body's immune system suddenly attacks the muscles of the heart, like those memorable comets that now and then flash across the night sky with a sudden and beautiful blazing brilliance and then all too quickly fade from our sight, our beloved little star boy had gone home. Need I speak to you of grief, you who've ever lost a loved one, most especially a child.

No. I didn't think so. It is for you that I've written this book.

Our longing for assurance that death is not an ending but in fact is a door into another dimension can be approached in several ways. One is the "OBE," the so-called "Out of Body Experience" which was famously experienced by the American author Ernest Hemingway in World War I and affected him so profoundly that it became a repeated event in his fiction. In July 1918, Hemingway, an ambulance driver, was delivering chocolate and cigarettes to Italian soldiers in the trenches near the front lines when an explosion knocked him unconscious, killed an Italian soldier, and blew the legs off another. Describing his experience, Hemingway wrote: "There was one of those big noises you sometimes hear at the front. I died then. I felt my soul or something coming right out of my body, like you'd pull a silk handkerchief out of a pocket by one corner. It flew all around and then came back and went in again and I wasn't dead any more."

Source: Wikimedia Commons

Hemingway.

Closely related to the OBE is the "NDE," the Near Death Experience that has been the subject of countless books. Billy Friedkin, who directed the film version of *The Exorcist*, many years ago told me that he had had one after a heart attack on the Hollywood Freeway in which paramedics had at first pronounced him dead. "Yeah, I heard the music, I was going through the tunnel toward the light, the whole thing," he told me quietly.

And another friend, Jack Tuero, my tennis teacher who was in the doubles finals at Forest Hills at the age of sixteen—he was famous for his devastating backhand—told me about his experience in a way that convinced me he wasn't "looking for attention," shall we say. I was living in Malibu at the time in a house that had a tennis court, and one day I invited the actor Bobby Duvall to come play tennis. He did and apparently had invited others, one of whom was the gorgeous Lynda Carter, the original TV "Wonder Woman." Anyway, Bobby was on the court and I was in the house talking about the NDE phenomenon to Lynda Carter and maybe someone else, but definitely Jack Tuero. Eventually Lynda, and whoever else was there, left the room, but Jack, who had been staring at me silently—and rather strangely—throughout my talk about the subject, just sat still and continued to do so. I can't remember my words, but I asked Jack if there was anything wrong, either that or something like, "What's the funny look for?" but his answer I recall precisely. First of all, he had never before heard of NDEs, and then went on to tell me in a haunted tone, "Well, I once had an experience like that." He'd had close to his entire stomach removed at the VA hospital in Sepulveda, California, he recounted, and while he was unconscious, he related, "I was in a room just off the Hospital Day Room. I could hear this—well, like organ music—and there were vets—patients— all around, they were all wearing hospital gowns out in the Day Room. Then I noticed three of them who looked different from the others. They were sitting on a gurney cart, but when I got closer to them I realized *they were sitting on my dead body!*" When I asked, "Did you tell any of the VA medics or surgeons about this?" Jack looked at me incredulously. "Bill," he said, "if I had I wouldn't ever have gotten out of there!"

While there have been neurological attempts to explain the NDE effect as being due to perfectly natural causes, Allan J. Hamilton, a Harvard educated neurosurgeon, in his book *The Surgeon and the Soul*, cites a relatively recent case in which these attempts at a materialist explanation are irrefutably rendered to be null and void. The patient, Sarah Gideon, a petite and pretty thirty-four-year-old, had undergone an extraordinary surgical procedure at the Barrow Neurological Institute in Scottsdale, Arizona, under the care of a Dr. Thomas Reed. The woman suffered from an intra-cranial cerebral hemorrhage caused by a basal tip aneurysm, and the only possible way to save her life involved cooling down her body temperature to below 90 degrees Fahrenheit at which point her heart would stop beating so that all blood flow to her body and brain would be cut off entirely caus-ing all brainwave activity to cease and thus rendering Gideon technically dead while the surgical team raced to repair the aneurysm, for they had a maximum of only twenty minutes in which to do so, or the patient's tem-porary death would be permanent. The operation was successful, and immediately upon reviving, without delay or opportunity to be in contact with the surgical team, the patient was audio and video taped while being subjected to questioning, in the course of which she recounted with perfect accuracy many things she had "seen" and "heard" during the course of the surgery, among them highly accurate and detailed descriptions of those in attendance, even of the location in the room of a heart lung bypass machine that had been wheeled in only after she had lost consciousness, and all of this corroborated by a playback of an audio recording that had been made from beginning to end of the surgery. Additionally, all of the doctors, nurses, and attendants involved in the surgery and its immediate aftermath were recorded on audio and video as well, so that there could be no question of mistaken or embroidered recollections. It was beyond dispute that Sarah Gideon's consciousness had been present in the operating theater even though it was not supported in any way by her brain.

There is also an argument for the soul expressed by a character in my aforementioned novel and film, *The Ninth Configuration*: "If we're nothing but atoms, just molecular structures no different in kind from this desk or this pen, then we ought to be always rushing blindly to serve our own self-ish ends. Then so how is there love in this world? I mean love as a God might love and a man will give his life for another?" Good question.

The best approach to healing grief is religious faith, even when for many believers "faith" is more accurately defined as "an intense hope."

And there's a powerful argument from reason, for we see that in nature, everywhere, always and without exception, there is never a case in which all of humanity has an inborn desire for something that neither exists nor can ever be attained. Without exception and in every time and every place, all humans have an inborn desire for perfect happiness. But this is something we know we can never attain, at least not here in the material universe, for we know that whatever measure of happiness we attain, it can never be perfect since we know that death will put an end to it. So unless we are willing to say that nature in this one-in-a-million case is either misinformed or willfully stupid, the question becomes not *when* we can attain perfect happiness, but *where*.

Very nice. Even fine. And after an early manhood that would likely stun even St. Augustine's mother, I am again a devoted, practicing Catholic who has studied all the rational, philosophical arguments for the immortality of the soul, and have precious little doubt that "Near Death Experiences" cannot be explained without positing that man is more than a collection of molecules. But where are all these arguments, these comforts, these supports, when you're looking down at your child in an open coffin at the mortuary "viewing" or when for over half an hour you are walking around and around the swimming pool in the basement of your home while loudly and tearfully shouting out over and over again, "*Peteeeyyyyyyyyy!!*" The grief, the searing ache of loss remains even when we believe there is really no death, because what is missing, I think, is the knowledge that our loved ones, as Cardinal Newman wrote, are not off somewhere having fun without us in a dark matter "Playland" some 17 billion light years away but in fact remain with us, are in communion with us, and that they see and hear us, and it is unrelenting evidence of the truth of this which is the gift that Peter has given to me and to Julie again and again over the past eight years and which I hope to be passing along to you. Don't expect tales of apparitions or of ghostly messages written on a mirror. No, this will not be *Ghostbusters Five*. Yes, a few of the "messages" do rise to a level that one—well, let's make that, that *I* could call proof. Most, though, when considered individually, might seem too subjective or to involve mere coincidence; however, when considered within the context of a constant repetition of such events—mostly those which are modest and in the few rare cases where they are borderline stunning over the course of so many years—they must be considered as evidential.

❯◆❮

As Petey's mother has been co-witness to so many of the "messages" from Pete, in terms of trusting her testimony you should know a few things about her. Born and raised in the western suburbs of Chicago, after seeing *The Red Shoes* on TV when she was only two, Julie became smitten, if not obsessed, with the idea of becoming a ballerina. She began ballet lessons at the age of four and began working as a professional singer, dancer, and actress at the age of nine, which is when she joined the National Company of *The Sound of Music* and toured with them for thirteen

First comes infestation, then obsession, then...

Totally gone, done, finished.

In the *Sound of Music* (second from right).

months as one of the Von Trapp children, and in later years appeared on stage in such classics as *Brigadoon, New Moon, Kismet, Steambath, The Man of La Mancha, Fiddler on the Roof,* and *A Funny Thing Happened on the Way to the Forum.*

It was yet another case of Providence handing me the Merry Go Round brass ring that in her early twenties Julie moved to Los Angeles where she was hired to be one of "The Embraceable Ewes," the original Los Angeles Rams cheerleaders. On April 20, 1980, we met on a blind date arranged by mutual friends. In 1983 we married and in 1987 and 1989 along came Peter and Paul, whom Julie home-schooled, teaching them, among other things, Latin and Greek, until they were in the seventh and ninth grades respectively. When we met, and all through the early years of our marriage, although born and raised a Roman Catholic, Julie had lost touch with her faith, but today is a Spiritual Director at Our Lady of Bethesda Retreat Center, leading me to feel, at times, like the male lead in an "A" rated version of *Thais.* So okay. Enough of that. But now how clear-eyed and objective an observer is she? Unfortunately, as you can see from the following photos—she's the one at extreme right in both—she's quite obviously an overly credulous, wide-eyed Miranda who will believe anything you tell her, goes to annual "Gaia" seminars in New Mexico, and thinks a Druid named Valerie founded San Francisco.

In the TV series *The Misadventures of Sheriff Lobo* (on the right).

And as an L.A. Rams cheerleader appearing on *The Tonight Show* with Johnny Carson (below) here she is leaping for joy upon hearing that the Dalai Lama has recovered from the flu.

Yes. Exactly.

"Gimme a 'D,' okay? And an ... "

Julie and George Burns watching someone levitate.

The Jerk, Sammy Cahn, Julie Blatty, and Tony Bennett at a meeting of the Beverly Hills "ghostly apparition society."

And now the messages from Pete. They began almost immediately, on the Tuesday night of Peter's death, in fact, when Julie had a remarkable "dream." So that it may come to you unfiltered and unedited, I have asked her to describe it for you:

The morning following Pete's death, I awakened very early after a fitful night. I lay in the darkness, too sad to weep, still numb, perhaps in shock. I remember looking at my bedside clock and seeing that it was nearly 7:00. Then I suddenly fell asleep. I dreamt that Bill and I were in a car, on our way to Our Lady of Bethesda, for a talk or presentation of some kind. I wasn't surprised that we were driving through a cloud filled sky. There were no other vehicles and the earth wasn't visible through the heavy clouds. Then in the distance, coming towards us, I saw a white pick-up truck. The windows were tinted and I couldn't see who was driving or if there was a passenger. Just before we were abreast of one another, I saw Peter coming through the windshield, although the glass did not break. I could also see at that point, that an angel was driving. In the dream, I felt no shock or surprise at seeing Peter in this unusual setting. In fact, I was filled with a deep sense of peace and a gentle curiosity. As I continued to watch Peter, I saw him lean forward and rest his large hands on the hood of the pickup. His beautiful long hair was flowing away from his face and the thought came to me that he looked like the figurehead on the prow of a great ship. He was wearing the same clothes he wore when he returned from Baltimore; a white T-shirt, jeans, and his gray corduroy jacket. I saw every detail of his appearance, as if in High-Def. His large hands, with their bruised knuckles, splayed out on the white hood, the Rosary Ring he wore around his neck on a chain, the tiny black dots of his beard, breaking through his fair skin, and the loving half smile on his lips. Then he began to sing. "Don't cry for me, I'm happy and I'm free," he sang. He continued to sing, smiling gently at me, and though I still heard the music I couldn't hear the words, not at all, and I knew he was singing about things I wasn't yet permitted to hear. Still, I was so comforted by his presence, and I knew—I *knew*—he was alive and where he was meant to be. I felt no urgency to cling to him, or to try to keep him with me. All was gentle, peaceful, serene. I awoke filled with that peace, believing God had answered my every prayer for Pete. Each night for the previous two years, I had begged God to heal his bipolar illness and free him from his addictions. Now I saw how those prayers had been answered. My soul was at rest. A couple of weeks after this experience, a family that Pete had grown close to in his final summer gave me a photo of Peter taken at the beach a few weeks before his death. I caught my breath when I saw it. It was my son, exactly as I had seen him in the dream, his hair flowing, the same enigmatic smile on his lips, and those beautiful, limpid eyes, gazing into eternity. Peter was home.

And again from Julie, her report of her experience of a night some weeks later:

As we got into bed, Bill and I touched hands and said, "One day closer"...our nightly exhortation to one another. It meant, "One day closer to Heaven." "One day closer to Peter." We turned away from one another to sleep, each curled up on our sides. Still far from sleep, I was praying silently when I began to experience the oddest sensation. I felt Peter's physical presence. I mean, I FELT PETER'S PHYSICAL PRESENCE! It was almost as if I were holding him tightly to my chest, and in fact, I crossed my hands over my heart and held him there. It was incredibly sweet, incredibly REAL, and I hardly dared breath, for fear it might desert me. I lay there for several delicious minutes, savoring it all, even as I wondered. It felt as if Peter's full grown essence had been compressed into a space about the size and shape of a small book. It wasn't even big enough to be the size of a newborn Pete, but I clung to him and felt all the love he was pouring into my soul. I loved him back with silent tears…tears of joy. Eventually the feeling began to wane, but just as with the dream, I didn't feel any urgency or sense that I wanted to cling to Pete, to keep him with me. All was peace.

Here (below) is the photo of Peter that Julie previously mentioned. It's the last one ever taken of him. We had a small, slim pillow measuring one foot by one foot with that photo imprinted on the face of it. What Julie didn't know at the time of her second dream of Pete is that on that same night I had fallen asleep tightly holding that pillow face-down on my chest

as I asked him to "come to me" in my sleep, so that when Julie recounted her experience to me, and thinking of the movie *Ghost* and the actress who had played the role of a clairvoyant, I said, "Julie, you're my Whoopi Gold-berg!"

The flow of strange events continued. On the night of Peter's passing, while alone in my study and seated at my desk, I fell apart, convulsed in sobbing, and as the tears began staunching their flow I heard clearly and distinctly from a point in the room about ten feet away and seemingly hovering above a long, tall bench that was covered with periodicals, the voice of a young man saying, "I love you." Did it sound just like Peter? Quite honestly, no, not unmistakably. But it was there, I heard it, it was real. While I will not make a habit of arguing for the validity of various phenomena as we go forward, here at the outset let me state that although my grief over Mama's passing was so deep and intense as to be considered neurotic and abnormal as it continued to weigh on my heart for almost five years, from the date of Mama's passing until this very moment I have never heard her disembodied voice nor has she ever given me—at least that I could see—even the slightest sign that she continued to exist.

Earlier that same day, something else very curious occurred. Peter's girlfriend, Charlotte Labeau, for whom Julie and I would later become her Catholic godparents, owned two miniature pug dogs, one black and one white, and the black one, named "Harry," with his head tilted upward began excitedly barking for about a full minute in the Labeaus' living room at—what?

Or was it "who"?

Still another odd happening that night involved a merry-hearted friend of Julie's named Judy DiGioia, a public school teacher who has always impressed me as not only quite intelligent but also as down to earth as a supermarket shopping cart. Peter was extremely fond of Judy. And so it hap-pened that on the evening of Peter's passing, she was kneeling in a small Catholic chapel for a devotion know as a "Holy Hour" in which Christ is on display in the form of a communion host in a monstrance on the center of the altar. Outside, a howling wind and heavy rainfall probably accounted for the fact that Judy was alone in the chapel, so that she felt free to pray aloud to Peter to give her a sign that he was happy. "I want an orange rose," she prayed, only to quickly correct the rose's color to red. Moments later, she said, she heard the sounds of the wind and rain grow suddenly louder as the heavy wooden front door was being opened, and then all was quiet again after it was closed. "And after that I heard something like cellophane crinkling," she told me and Julie, and then heavy-footed galoshes squishing and thumping as someone came down the aisle toward her and the altar. Judy lifted her head from prayer, she told us, to see a tall and heavy-set woman advancing toward the altar holding high in her hand a long-stemmed red rose. Strapped over her shoulder was a large bright orange leather bag. The woman placed the rose in a flower holder on the altar, then stepped back and prostrated herself face-down on the ground before the exposed Sacred Host.

The next day, a Wednesday, as I half-dozed in a deep-cushioned chair, in the split second preceding my full awakening, I saw—not in the room but as if implanted on the surface of my eyes—Peter and someone else with him. Smiling, they were kneeling in front of me. Peter was wearing a pale blue sweater. There wasn't time for me to tell who the other person was, but I had the definite and very strong impression that Peter was trying to cheer me up and to assure me that all was well. Subjective? Oh, of course, very possibly, I suppose. But not so with what came next.

It was the next day, Thursday. Standing alone somewhere in the house, I was reflecting on Judy DiGioia's tale of the rose when I found myself saying in a firm, loud voice, "Pete, I want a sign of my own. I want a rose. I want—" And here I mentally stumbled, pondering what color the rose should be, then, unthinking, I blurted out, "I want a blue rose!" Nothing had changed, you see, from the days when I would lock myself out of my beer truck and couldn't solve the Einsteinean equations for the proper operation of a child's pedal-car, since even at the age of seventy-eight I had no clue that in nature blue roses did not exist. And so every time flowers of condolence arrived at the house, I kept hopelessly looking for this floral unicorn until one day—whether in a dream or while awake I can't recall—I awakened with a sense, a premonition, you could say, that I would receive my blue rose at Gate of Heaven, the cemetery where Peter was to be interred in an above-ground mausoleum vault. On the day before the burial mass and the burial, Father John Hopkins, a priest of the order of the Legionaries of Christ, had said to me and Julie, "Tomorrow will be a celebration, right?" I had nodded in assent. It was a lie.

The next day, Sunday, after emerging from the limo at the cemetery, I found myself absently walking ahead of Julie and Father Hopkins toward the site of Peter's burial enclosure when to my right and about shoulder height I came upon a burial vault that was decorated with a spray of artificial flowers. I stopped and my heart began to flutter: The flowers were red, white, and blue. When Julie and Father Hopkins caught up with me, I said, "Look at these flowers, Julie." She said, "Why?" I had told her nothing of my request for a "sign." "Just tell me, are they roses?" I said. Julie looked at the bouquet and said, "No. They're carnations." Then her brow wrinkled up as she leaned in her head for a closer look, and "No," she said, "I'm wrong. Yes, they are. They're roses." God knows what expression Julie and the priest saw on my face, but I walked away rapidly back to the curb of the street where I erupted with peal after peal of laughter. No words. Just the loud and continuous laughter, and though at the time it hadn't occurred to me, "Blessed are they who mourn for they will laugh" does now come to mind. It turns out that the day I'd asked Petey to give me a blue rose, Thursday, November 11th, was Veteran's Day, and so now will Richard Dawkins and the epiphenomenalist police stamp their feet in a pout like Dulcy and then tar, feather, and stone me for daring to raise the possibility that Peter had foreseen that I'd find a placement of "blue roses" on the day of his interment and that it was not I who chose the color blue for my rose but Peter who had wafted it into my mind? To be fair, in the case of the many less dramatic "signs and messages" Julie and I are convinced that Peter has given us, a selection of which I will recount, the materialists do have a point. But as I've mentioned before, in the context of the few clearly astounding events, and the frequent, if not constant, occurrence of the lesser ones over the course of so many years, it seems to me quite fair to believe that the case for coincidence dwindles.

And so now, at times from notes but mostly from memory, here, uncolored by opinionating—oh, well, I'll do my best, okay?—and in no particular order, are some other of the events that Julie and I have taken to be messages of comfort from Peter, though of course you are to make of them whatever you will.

PETEY'S MEDAL

Much of the last two months of Peter's life were spent with a friend and the parents of the friend at Hilton Head in South Carolina, which is also where that last photo of Peter was taken. At the public showing at the mortuary, the friend's father handed me a silvery medallion. "Peter asked if he could have it," the friend's father told me, "but he left it behind when he went back home." I looked down at the medallion. It bore the imprint of the three crosses on Calvary, with the two on the outside leaning in toward the one in the center. At the funeral mass the next day I noticed that the devotional pamphlet containing the day's gospel passage bore the same image that was on the medallion with the two outer crosses of Calvary tilting sharply inward. This is not how they are usually depicted.

Within days I attached the medallion to a silvery chain which, except for going through security at airports, I have never taken off to this day. Yet off it did come on one occasion and in a very baffling way. In May 2007, about a week before I was to give a speech at a dinner hosted by the American Task Force For Lebanon, I awakened to find that my medallion chain was loose at both ends and Peter's medal was missing. I searched the bedding, I searched under and all around the bed, I searched my completely glassed-in shower stall. Nothing. Julie then joined the search and over and over again we kept searching my shower stall and the area both under and on top of our bed. Still nothing. A day or two later as I showered I declared aloud firmly—and I remember it word for word—"Petey's going to find that medal for me." It was so important to me. I loathe public speaking, always fearful of a repetition of the "Thomas Jefferson" fiasco, and I wanted the medal found for moral support. As I showered on the morning of the day I was to give the speech, when I happened to glance down at the shower floor I was puzzled to see, beneath a half inch of water and soapy bubbles, something shiny and reflecting light from the shower's overhead light bulb. I turned off the water, bent down, and picked it up. It was Petey's medal.

Let's go over it again: the glassed-in, brightly lit shower stall measured a little less than four feet by four feet. Julie and I had separately entered the shower and meticulously searched it in broad daylight at least three times, in my case I think at least five. As a test, then, and recalling that the medal was larger than a twenty-five cent coin and of a smooth and shiny silvery metal, one day soon after my speech I placed a copper penny that was dulled with age at the same spot in my shower where I'd found the medal. I then

Gospel   Luke 23:33, 39-43

When the soldiers came to the place called the Skull, they crucified Jesus and the criminals there, one on his right, the other on his left.

Now one of the criminals hanging there reviled Jesus, saying, "Are you not the Messiah? Save yourself and us."

The other man, however, rebuking him, said in reply, "Have you no fear of God, for you are subject to the same condemnation?

And indeed, we have been condemned justly, for the sentence we received corresponds to our crimes, but this man has done nothing criminal."

Then he said, "Jesus, remember me when you come into your kingdom."

He replied to him, "Amen, I say to you, today you will be with me in Paradise."

The Gospel of the Lord   R./ *Praise to you, Lord Jesus Christ*

Today You Will Be With Me In Paradise!

Remembrance pamphlet at Peter's funeral mass.

invited Julie to come into my bathroom and check to see whether there was anything unusual on the shower floor. She looked, shook her head, and said, "No," and then pointing she added, "There's just that penny over there."

TURNING ON A LIGHT

After Peter's death, Julie and I found that the empty hours between the end of dinner and bedtime were when the undistracted mind was most susceptible to spasms of sad remembrance and of grief, and so we began a custom of filling those hours with watching television miniseries, the most distracting having homicide themes, *Prime Suspect* for example, the more serial killings the better. On a night approximately three years ago, we were watching an episode of that kind of show entitled *New Tricks* that featured a tall, leggy blonde as the "DCI," the lead detective, with three more detectives working under her command. Upon the death of his wife, one of these detectives had her buried in the back yard of their home, and every night he would get drunk and, sitting on a bench facing her gravestone, he would talk to her aloud. On this particular episode of the series, while thus engaged, he calls out loudly, "Sarah, why don't you ever give me a sign? Why don't you turn on a light or something?" On a fireplace mantel to my right there was a photo of Pete, and because at this point we had received so many "signs" from him, my glance immediately went to that photo, and then from there to a four-globe chandelier that overlooks our television watching area. I remember wryly smiling as I shook my head a little and thought, "My God, if Petey were to turn on a light in this room right now I think I'd levitate up to the ceiling like a sparrow!" I put it out of my mind. But then fifteen seconds later Julie and I found ourselves turning our heads to stare at one another, for except for the glow from the television screen and a little from the computer on my desk far behind us, up until that moment the room had been totally dark. Then, looking to the left, we saw that a halogen lamp atop one of my filing cabinets had come on, and, without any trace of flickering, its light remained full and steady for about twenty seconds before silently going out. Julie and I got up and in silence we went over to inspect the lamp. It was Julie who observed that the "rocker" switch used for turning the lamp on and off was in the "off" position. What can I say? This house measures ten thousand square feet of interior space and in the fourteen years that we have lived in it, not one other time have we ever observed an incandescent light to turn itself on.

The next day, and doubtless due to my intense desire that Peter was responsible for the light coming on, I spent some time as either "Doubting Thomas" or Inspector Clouseau—I leave the choice to you—I started out by theorizing that perhaps Julie was mistaken and the rocker switch had *not* been off when the lamp came on, but then in testing the switch I discovered that now the lamp would not turn on no matter the position of the switch. I changed the bulb. Nothing. The lamp was "over." Dead. And so what we were dealing with here was a malfunctioning mechanism, I miserably concluded, ignoring the fact that if so the lamp had chosen an astoundingly coincidental moment for its final swan song.

Then came that night. Our miniseries viewing over, Julie picked up the cat to take it up to its nightly lair while I sat down in my desk chair to check my computer for late e-mails. Once again, every light in the room was off when I noticed a flaring of light reflected in my computer screen and, swiveling around, I saw that the light was coming from the four-globe chandelier above the TV viewing area that my gaze had gone to the night before! And this is what I saw: imagine, if you will, someone manipulating a dimmer switch as very, very slowly, the globes go from total darkness to full illumination, then very, very slowly down to full darkness again. *This happened two more times.* As usual, you are free to assess all of this for yourselves, but if you will forgive the editorial intrusion, my interpretation of the event at the time was, *"Dad, you need a building to fall on top of you?!"*

NOAH'S TREE

Remember the tree in our backyard that Peter's friend Noah had planted as a memorial to Peter's loyalty and courage? Standing out on the back deck of our home a couple of weeks after Petey's passing, my hands in pockets, I said aloud, "Petey, give me a hug," when suddenly a soft breeze arose wafting autumn leaves straight into my chest just like that dollar bill long, long ago. The next thing I remember is that, staring at Noah's tree I thought, "Now what if it were to bloom on my birthday, *that* would *truly* be a sign!" If not a miracle, for my birthday is January 7. And of course you know what's coming, which is that day, in the thick of a Maryland winter, *green shoots sprouted out all over Noah's tree*! Forgive the italics: I was recapturing my excitement of that moment. The sprouts never flowered, and from that day forward Noah's tree began a slow death.

THE "PEEP"

Over the course of time, the aforementioned Judy DiGioia began having more "experiences" of Peter, the most striking being what she told us occurred late in the morning on Easter Saturday 2007. She was sick with the flu and in bed, she said, could not get the TV in her bedroom to work, and at some point, while feeling drowsy, she talked aloud to Peter, saying, "Peter, I want you to give me a sign that you're happy and that you're looking after my family." She told Peter that the sign was to be a "Peep," one of those marshmallow, yellow-coated candy confections in the shape of a chick used primarily to fill Easter baskets. On becoming more wakeful, however, Judy regretted her choice of a peep for a sign inasmuch as she and everyone in her family "detested"—her word—the confection and the chances of anyone bringing one into her household that day was nil. Then her husband Greg came home. He repaired the TV and when he'd left the room, Judy, finding her Kleenex box empty, got up and retrieved the one at her husband's side, then got back into bed, blew her nose, picked up the remote, and turned on the TV to catch a flashing image of President Obama's former pastor, the Reverend Wright, before the TV screen went to black for perhaps a second and then came back on again just in time for Judy to see a blonde news anchor with a large Easter basket on a table beside her holding out her hand to Judy with something yellowish in it while saying cheerily, "And here's a peep for *you!*"

And now, in July of 2014, as I type these words I have an unexpected update to this incident. Last night, Julie Blatty and I and our son Paul were invited to a Mexican dinner at the home of the Catholic Consecrated Women of *Regnum Christi*, a young and faith-filled, vivacious group who, though not nuns, have taken vows of poverty, chastity, and obedience. As we sat at table over dessert, Julie recounted for them "the tale of the peep." On the day of the dinner, unknown to these women as well as to Julie, I had stood in front of a photo of Pete and asked him to be present at the dinner. Today, Julie received the following e-mail from Jacqueline Gonzalez, a pretty, dark-eyed member of the consecrated women who had cooked the dinner:

——————— Forwarded message ———————

From: **González Jacqueline** (e-mail address deleted)
Date: Fri, Apr 4, 2014 at 10:57 AM
Subject: Peep!!!!
To: Julie Blatty (e-mail address deleted)

Dearest Julie,

Seriously what a joyful time we had last night!!! Thank you so much!!! We have the best family!!!! God is good!!!

Ok, you are not going to believe this.... it's pretty incredible ... last night after the dinner we were at the kitchen cleaning up and we realized that one of our missionaries had brought home 1 left over donut I guess from her LTP meeting.... I am attaching the pictures of the donut so that you see what we all saw last night!!!!

We seriously wanted to cry since to me it was a miraculous sign that Peter was present at the dinner last night and that he is so happy to see the 3 of you together enjoying life!!!!!! He is very grateful for all the love each of you has for him ...

Please share this with Bill and Paul :-) maybe another story for his book!!!

I am still in shock.... there are no coincidences ... only perfect moments planned by the loving heart of God!!!

Big hug, JG

Make of this what you will, but as for me I am thinking, "So what else is new?" Meantime, here is the photo attached to Jacqueline Gonzalez's e-mail:

The Peep that came to dinner.

A photo of us taken after the dinner:

The women, Paul, and Julie. Jacqueline is the girl I am hugging.

A "COINCIDENCE" IN SALEM

A super skeptic generally, and in particular when I told him about one or two of the things I'm relating to you here, my sixty-year-old son Michael has long been a hard-case doubter of things that go bump in the night or in Macy's window at the stroke of noon for that matter. Yet on what would have been Peter's twenty-first birthday, some whim, some sentiment, some sudden impulse possessed Mike to do something he hadn't done in years, which was to attend a Catholic mass in Salem, Massachusetts, where he was living at that time. Afterwards he called me to recount that at the mass, following the gospel reading and before delivering the homily, the priest had asked the congregation whether there was anyone in attendance whose birthday it was. A young man in his twenties raised his hand. The priest asked him his name and the young man said, "Peter." It was around this time that Mike's wife, Marion, called to tell me that she had had a very brief but intensely lucid dream of Peter. "There he was," she said, "and I said, 'Peter, are you alright?' and he just laughed and hugged me."

THE LOST ROSARY

Within a few months after Peter's death, I attended mass at Blessed Sacrament in Chevy Chase, the church we always attended and where Peter's funeral mass had been held. I had taken Peter's rosary beads with me. That night, after taking off my pants and removing their contents and placing them on my bathroom counter, I was mildly panicked to find that Peter's rosary was missing. I made a new search of the trouser pockets, then another. Nothing. Gone. I had a restless sleep. On awakening, I made another fruitless search of my trouser pockets, thoroughly searched the floor beneath which they'd been hanging, and then drove to Blessed Sacrament where I asked if a rosary had turned up in Lost and Found. The answer was no, but I was told that the head of the cleaning crew would be back after evening devotions that night and he would know better, so that night I returned to the church, talked to the head of the cleaning crew, and once again came up empty. Angry at myself for taking the rosary out of the house in the first place, I maniacally pulled the trousers' pockets inside out, again found nothing and then finally gave up. I slept in a bit the next morning and was awakened by Julie's voice saying, "Sweetie?" I opened my eyes. In one hand she was holding my trousers and in the other Peter's rosary. In a mildly perplexed tone of voice, she said, "Bill, I found Petey's rosary." I said, "Really? Where was it?" and she answered, "In your pants pocket."

SUNFLOWERS

Pete's favorite flower was the sunflower. I drink coffee from a cup that commemorates that fact. It's dark blue with three sunflowers on its outer shell. On the Saturday just before Mother's Day 2013, I stood before an enlarged photo of Peter that hangs on my office wall, and I said, "Petey, tomorrow's Mother's Day. Could you maybe do something really personal for your Mom?" I made an online "Open Table" reservation for brunch the next day at The Daily Grill in Bethesda. On the website you could order flowers delivered to your table and I chose a modest one entirely comprised of Gerbera daisies, and when we got to our table, there, indeed, were the flowers. Around the perimeter were Gerbera daisies but the preponderance of the flowers, all clustered in the center, were a clutch of vividly bright and beautiful sunflowers. Sunflowers are much more expensive than Gerbera daisies. Had the florist run out of them, wouldn't he have filled in the order with less expensive flowers, plain daisies for example? I mention this only in passing. In the meantime, something else involving sunflowers happened. In my novel *Dimiter*, an Arab policeman in Jerusalem who is grieving over the loss of a very young son, places a paper bookmark in a book about the afterlife he's been reading and when he returns to reading it, the bookmark is no longer there and in its place is the dead son's favorite flower, a sunflower. I'm sorry, I can't give you the date or the other persons involved, only that about three years ago after Julie and I had been discussing something about my novel *Legion* with friends, we drifted into my study where, intending to reinforce a point I had made with something in the novel's text, I slipped a copy of it off a bookshelf when out from its pages fell a dried out sunflower. Can I swear on Mama's grave that I hadn't placed it there? No, I can't. But I can also swear that I had not—and have not to this day—the slightest recollection of ever placing it there. Along the lines of this modest type of event, there are many relating to the fact that we live on the edge of a forest where on rare occasions, perhaps once, sometimes twice a year, we might see a family of deer passing by. Call us grasping at straws if you will, but Julie and I tend to believe that Peter has many times produced their appearance for us on demand. I have a written notation, in fact, dated "January 14, 2009," Julie's birthday. On the day before, the note reminds, she had asked him for a birthday gift of a sighting of deer, and now, in the morning of that day, I'm the first one down to the kitchen where immediately I look out at the forest but see no deer, which at that time of year would be highly visible since the trees were all barren of leaves. Disappointed, I sit at the kitchen table with my back to the woods. Julie appears, asks me what I'd like for breakfast, then gasps as, wide-eyed and happy, she stares out at the forest and "Oh, look!" she exclaims, "A deer!" In fact, a family of four. They are all in a resting position, appearing to be looking back at us, and remain so for about *two hours*. Yes, I know, a single blossom doesn't make a spring nor a single hair a beard, but over the years I have observed Petey to oblige with this particular request many times and, more important, has never failed to do so.

BEDTIME PRAYERS

Before Peter crossed over, he and his little brother Paul would kneel at the end of our bed every night to say their prayers. A week or two after the funeral, I started saying my nightly prayers in Pete's room. Kneeling at the end of his bed, I repeat the nightly bedtime recitations of the child's prayer beginning, "Now I lay me down to sleep, I pray the Lord my soul to keep," then another prayer that begins, "Angel of God, my guardian dear," these along with my own nightly prayers. A couple of things happened relating to this practice. The first was about two weeks after I'd started this ritual, my daughter Mary Jo called me from Los Angeles to tell me, with a certain urgency in her voice, that after feeling inexplicably "impelled" to start going through her daughter Jessica's childhood letters and files, she had found a letter to Jessica from Peter and that on the outside of the envelope Jessica had written in pencil, "Now I lay me down to sleep" and that for some reason she couldn't explain, Mary Jo felt it was somehow important that she tell me about it. At my request she mailed the letter to me. The inscription on the outside of the envelope was as she had described it to me, while in the body of the letter Peter writes out the prayers he advises Jessica to say at night, the "Now I lay me down to sleep" and the one to the guardian angel.

Something else about Peter's bedroom. Well into his teens, he'd retained possession of a tiny stuffed puppy dog about the size of a grown man's hand. He'd named it "Pup-Pup" and slept with it every night of his life until, the year before his passing, we had to place Peter in Suburban Hospital for a couple of days of examination because of symptoms that were at last confirmed to be of bipolar disorder type one. We made the mistake of bringing Pup-Pup with him. When we checked Petey out, "Pup-Pup" was missing from his hospital room, stolen, I suspect, by the deeply disturbed and ever spookily silent young teenager who was Peter's hospital roommate. The loss seemed to deepen Peter's constant sadness and depression. I remember him laying atop the covers on his bed in his room at home and looking off sadly as he said to me quietly, "Dad, 'Pup-Pup' was my childhood," a period of his life that he more than once had told me and Julie was "perfect." I offered a substantial cash reward to the Suburban Hospital's fourth floor staff for Pup-Pup's return, but nothing resulted other than an offering by a worker in the hospital's laundry facility of a freshly manufactured miniature stuffed puppy. The sales tag was still on its leg. Then something happened. One night after saying prayers in Pete's bedroom, I decided to stay and soak up memories for a while. The room was, and remains, exactly as Peter had left it without the loss or addition of so much as the books on his bedside table. I sat down in a rocking chair by Pete's bed and because there had already been so many things that we had taken to be "messages" from Pete, my very first thought, as I precisely recall it, was along the lines of, "Oh, if only 'Pup-Pup' would turn up somewhere, somehow, someday, what a sign *that* would be!" Then *immediately*—I swear to you—when my gaze drifted over to the various stuffed animals we kept up against the bed's pillows, I was surprised to see something new there. I got up, walked over to it, and picked it up. About the size of "Pup-Pup," it was a stuffed Humpty Dumpty with a winding key in its back that played a Humpty Dumpty theme. Julie happened to be in her office, which is adjacent to Petey's bedroom, and I walked in and showed it to her. "What's this?" I asked, and "Oh, that's 'Humpty,'" she said. "Humpty was Petey's original Pup-Pup."

MY DREAMS OF PETE

While I can't place these dreams in time, their content remains vivid and clear.

1) I see Pete entering my view, coming out of one room in our house and crossing left to right to another. He is shoeless and midway across he steps one of his feet into one of his shoes and his other foot into the other. I am puzzled by what I see as an unusual action, and when I've awakened and come down for breakfast I mention it to Julie who tells me, "Oh, that's always how Pete got into his shoes." Call me oblivious, if you will, but as I was never around when Pete dressed, I suppose, I had never seen him do this.

2) I am outdoors. I see Pete walking up the stairway of an underground subway kiosk. He is smiling. And then in another such dream I see Pete's bare legs sticking out from under the hatch door of either a hearse

or an ambulance type of vehicle. He is dead. But I place my hands on his legs and they are warm. Were these dreams Freudian wishes or messages from Pete? I don't know.

3) It is December 7, 2011. I am—asleep? dreaming? I'm not sure. I'm in bed on my back staring up at Pete as he leans over to give me a hug and says, "Happy Birthday, Dad." If it was a dream it was of the kind they call "lucid," it seemed so real and its cause could have been my conscious or unconscious desire. Except for one little problem: My birthday is not December 7. It's *January* 7.

CAT MISCHIEF

This late 2013 event risks eliciting a smirk, though in the context of everything else it still brings me a smile of bemusement along with a gentle shaking of the head in wonderment. In his younger years, Peter's brother Paul had a pet cat he'd named Boo-Boo. Though Paulie now lives on his own, the cat remains, and one early morning about half past one it awakened us with mews and muted howlings from the finished attic area above our bedroom. Julie got up out of bed and spent at least twenty minutes upstairs trying to coax the cat out from where she seemed trapped inside the attic walls, a place that she'd previously entered and left twice before without need of a GPS. This time was different. Julie finally gave up and got back into bed. But the mewlings of distress went on and on until around two-fifteen, two-thirty, at which point Julie jumped out of bed again and went into her bathroom to stand directly under the spot from which the mewlings were emanating, and after a few moments I heard her irritably and loudly declare, "Petey, can't you get into the head of this freaking cat! I want her out of the attic meowing at our bedroom door in no more than half a minute!" Alright, brace yourselves. Fine, call me a liar or a Lebanese Scheherazade spinning and embellishing a story. Sure, go ahead! Try it! But *immediately* after Julie's exasperated command to Pete, we heard the sudden clumping cat feet running above us and in less than

a minute, Boo-Boo—God, how that name hurts this story!—was meowing for entry at our bedroom door! Okay, now think about it: If this didn't
really happen, don't you think I'm a good enough writer of fiction to come
up with something far more dramatic and far less a potential giggle-
maker? Silence. Nevertheless, I report, you decide.

Meantime, here's more for your possible sneers of derision. I've told
you how I say my nightly prayers in Peter's bedroom. Well, that's where
the cat is kept at night, and ever since Paul struck out on his own two years
ago, whenever I enter and kneel at the foot of Pete's bed, the cat apparently
thinks that I've come to visit, if not worship, *her*, and is constantly and
annoyingly purring and meowing while repeatedly rubbing the bottom
of her chin on my prayer-folded hands, this followed by her rubbing her
entire body against my face, and then turning her back on me with her
butt two inches from my face in hopes of God knows what reciprocal
action on my part, then comes over and flops down atop my wrists. The
cat had been doing this without a single exception for almost seven years.
But after Julie's experience with Boo-Boo, as I entered Peter's room one
night and the cat was as usual meowing and purring and prancing about
like a total cat fool, I irritably asked Pete aloud to keep her away from me
while I prayed. And what happened next? *This*: The cat jumped up atop
the bed, made a beeline for my knuckles as usual, but then lifted her head,
holding motionless for a few seconds while staring straight ahead at noth-
ingness before abruptly turning and soundlessly padding away to a point
on the bed about two feet away from me, flopped down in a resting position, front claws tucked under her chest like some feline Wannabe Sphinx
and then stayed there, never even so much as glancing my way even after,
prayers ended, I got up and left the room. Except for a variation in which
the cat doesn't move away from me but remains sitting on its haunches
staring steadily ahead at who knows what, ever since then the pattern has
been as follows: On an average of three nights per week, the cat keeps its
distance as just described, while on the other nights it's the same old
annoying, slobbering, catfanticide-inducing routine. I've come to welcome

it, in fact, for it helps me to tell when Pete is actually present so that after prayers on these occasions I sit in the rocking chair and for a while I talk to him. Afterwards, I always feel better.

"PEE-WEE"

I could go on with so very many more of what Julie and I are convinced are interactions with Pete, but as they are mostly of the less dramatic kind—awakening in bed with the strong scent of Petey's favorite aftershave flooding your nostrils, for example—they are often subjective and, more important, tend to get repetitive. Further, there's simply no need to recount all of the "incidents" to make the point. Nevertheless, I will detail for you the very latest—what shall I call it? odd coincidence? I'll leave it to you. It happened only six weeks ago. Julie and a girlfriend met for lunch at the Woodmont Grill in Bethesda. Across the street there is a parking garage, and on this particular day stretched out on the sidewalk in front of it, his back against the wall, lay a red-bearded, sturdy-looking homeless man in his fifties, perhaps his early sixties, and on seeing him, Julie told her friend that it reminded her of her fear that, because of his bipolar illness, had he lived Peter too might very likely have wound up a homeless person, whereupon, and *instantly*, the homeless man raised his hand and out of nowhere loudly declared, "My birthday is May 17!" When Julie stopped dead in her tracks with a dumbfounded stare and her lady friend asked what was wrong and Julie answered that May 17 was Peter's birthday, the lady friend freaked. Who wouldn't! Since that incident, and finding that this homeless person had set up camp at the top of an exterior stairway by the parking garage, I've sought him out and engaged him in conversation. He won't give me his name; he says I can call him "Pee-Wee" after the memorable Brooklyn Dodgers shortstop Pee-Wee Reese. I asked him his birthday and he confirmed it was May 17. I also asked him what had prompted him to shout that out at Julie and her friend and he said that he didn't remember doing that.

And there you have it, "just the facts." Or a few of them. Would that all I've here recorded were as strikingly dramatic and with Special Effects as it was with the Turning on of the Light, but what I've here recorded, except for scores of repetitive little incidents, are all that there have been to date.

While riding in Joe Paterno's funeral cortege a couple of years ago, in a seat behind me was one of Joe's cousins, Joan Emrich, who was still deeply mourning the loss of a son and to whom I had tried to give comfort by telling her one or two things about Peter. I'd also urged her to "talk to your son, he hears you, Joan," just as I'd told Sue Paterno, Joe's grieving widow, to "talk to Joe," which she does, she has told me, every morning and night. Only last week I received a letter from Joan (see Exhibit "A" on page 205) informing me that she had experienced "three major" and many "minor" contacts with her son and wanted to thank me for helping her deal with her grief, which is all I've been trying to do here, as best I can, for all of you burdened with that wound that never heals, the loss of a loved one, most especially if it's your child and in that regard, and parenthetically, let me quote, and commend to your will, a very striking line that is uttered by a psychic in the movie, *The Orphanage*: "First you must believe. *Then* you will see."

Very well then. We're done. Would that I could claim that my impulse to help all those who mourn is some Lebanese version of the "milk of human kindness," because mostly it isn't; rather it's my hope that it will one day provide me with "Narrow Gate Grease." In the meantime, I assure you that I haven't made up a single word of this narrative, for if I had, as a writer of fiction, I could have made up far more dramatic incidents of Peter's "messaging." Further, "to help your unbelief," please know that every penny of royalties earned by this book goes directly to scholarships established in Peter's name at his former high school, The Heights in

Potomac, Maryland, to which you may also wish to contribute. In the meantime, since you've stayed with me up to this point, can I take it that you believe all I've told you? That would be nice.

THE END

EXHIBIT "A"

Dear Bill Blatty —

I continue to read your inspirational words to me — They mean so much —

I, too, have had very concrete messages from my beloved Michael — unbelievable signs — three major and many small — I seem to go looking for him — I read by hanging on to him — I'm holding his spirit back — which is disturbing but — I continue to search for him! I know he's here with me.

I wanted you to know — my very deepest gratitude to you —

June (Orrick)

EXHIBIT "B"

Notes that I worked from while writing *The Exorcist* novel appear on the following pages.

SYMPTOMS

ADVANCED IN STORY:
RAPPINGS
1. Face and voice changes   2. Spirit writing on flesh
3. Glossolalia   4. Levitation
5. ESP   6. Move objects at a distance
7. Produce odors   8. LOUDNESS of the voice

---

1. HYPER-MOTOR ACTIVITY
   A. Flung about and tossed on bed into air.
   B. Mewing, hissing, barking, neighing
   C. Produce body odors: MENTALLY ILL CAN DO THIS . Process
unconscious but some reported able to control production.
   D. Anelgesia: insensitivity to pain (while clawing face)
It occurs spontaneously in case of hysterics and hypnotic subjects.
   E. "Oh, my God, oh, my God!" and "I burn
   F. Head being shaken and tossed.
   G. Great bodily strength involved in the motor excitement,
which is itself indication of pathological state (in other words,
patient not faking the motor activity).
   H. Head twisted, tongue hangs far out of mouth, body bent
backwards like a bow, so that feet touch head. Wrestler's
bridge in the nude. Disordered agitation of the limbs, with
contortions and dislocations in the most impossible directions.
Such actions as a rule cannot be executed voluntarily.
   I. Case histories agree strength of several people needed to
restrain fitsx and hold patients.
   J. Children immediately dominated, because their personalities
not strong enough.
   K. Final breakout is a hideous, yelping laugh.
   L. Howlings and cries. Body rigid as if in grip of tetanus.
Lower extremities crossing and uncrossing, arms turned backwards
as if twisted. Head thrown side to side or far back, revealing
a swollen, bulging throat. Face depicts now fright, now anger, and
sometimes madness. Turgescent and purple. Eyes widely open,
fixed or rolled in their sockets, generally showing only the
white of the sclerotic. Lips parted and drawn in opposite
directions, showing a protrudig and tumified tongue. If fright
dominates, head inclined toward neck and thorax. Two clenched
hands clutched eyes and forehead tightly. Drawn faces and haggard
eyes. Body huddled up. Either lays to one side or on face,
with legs doubled up under abdomen or hiding hands in face. If
anger in the ascendant, throws self on obstacle and tries to
seize or bite it. TEARS OWN HAIR, scratches face and bosom. Crying
in pain and rage!
   M. Hiccupping. Ikota. and Africa
   N. SHE hears RAPPINGS at first when NO ONE ELSE DOES.
   O. GLACIAL COLD   P. SLEEPING FITS AFTER ATTACKS!

Expos. in Satan. Also, skin-writing. Prison psychiatrist a few
years ago described a prisoner who, in self-induced trance,
could cause the signs of the zodiac to appear and disappear
on his flesh... ZODIAC KILLER???

VOMITING BILE / "ANIMAL
CLASSICAL DANCING / NO EATING

"POSSESSED"

THE PLACE: WASHINGTON, D.C.

TIME: THE PRESENT.

THE MOTHER: is Shirley MacLaine. Hollywood High grad,
former actress. Auditioned on every producer's couch in
town. Married a callow youth who abandoned her and the
children when he made it on a TV series called "Surfside
Six." She came to Washington, took a secretarial ⌐ course
and is working for a Senator. Her husband died in Vietnam.
She loved him and hoped he come out of his temporary insanit
She is incredibly bright and self-educated through xxxx
omnivorous reading. She's having an affair with the Senato
(with a college boy on the side) because she's despaired
of human love. She loves the violin and xxxxxx had her
son Jamie take lessons. (later⌐, Paganini).
She has seduced at least one priest in her lifetime.

THE PRIEST: has lost his faith. He needs a sign. He is
not of the order of exorcists. He teaches clinical
psychology at Georgetown. The exorcism is a torture for him
He is illegitimate, his father a pimp, his mother a hooker.
He took the cloth like "The Prisoner". But he is a truly
good man, conscientious and sensitive, nagged by duty and
conscience, his unbelief in some part the result of axxx
subconscious desire to be released from his nagging,
"scrupulous" conscience. He had a wild boyhood in the
Lower East Side of New York. He is Italianxxbxxn-on-his--
mother's-side,-Jewish--- Irish (mother) -Italian (father).

"Can't we ever rest?!" ------ He attended college on
scholarship, left in mid-senior year to join the Jesuits
He is incredibly susceptible to owmen, has dreaming fantasies
This above all tortures his conscience and is his hangup.
The intellectual problem is a rationalization.

Through the cynicism shines through -- terribly -- an
innocence and sensitivity -- almost naivete -- that, onc
One has restrained the impulse to laugh,-is startlingly
moving.
What is he fighting? GUILT. The intellectual manifestation is
loss of faith.
He is also a reformed alcoholic. Kazantzakis' "last Temptatior
Th--recalls Christ with grandchildren......

TERRY AND THE WEREWOLF

by

William Peter Blatty

AS ONCE SUBMITTED TO THE

SATURDAY EVENING POST

N ow maybe you'll think it strange that I should have been pouring coffee for the brown-eyed daughter of the New York City Police Commissioner just like I was a waiter or something and it could be you'd be right except actually you'd be wrong inasmuch as at the time I *was* a waiter and everyone I waited on at this Catskill Mountains summer resort was either a New York policeman or somebody in his family. The resort was owned and managed by the New York City Police Department so I guess the whole thing was real proper and I'm sorry if I worked you up over nothing but I still get a little muddle-headed when I think of that time I first met Terry.

"You are somewhat late for breakfast, Miss," I said to her really warm like.

"You're pouring black coffee into my bran flakes," she answered me, possibly even more warm like. I mean, you'd expect she'd be ticked or something but when she looked up at me with that twinkly half question, half smile in her eyes, I felt something in my head go "crunch," although maybe that's how bran flakes react to hot coffee but that didn't occur to me at the time, I just felt that I'd fallen into like, which was good, but then we had the werewolf hunt, which was not.

And of course there was waiter Gregg Malloy.

Malloy had the looks of a young Greek god just finished with his junior year at Cambridge, and though there was indeed something other-worldly about the way he handled his section of the dining room, he was unfortu-nately no myth. He also had an altogether earthly interest in the aforemen-tioned eighteen-year-old Miss Harnedy.

"I have an interest in your new guest, a Miss Harnedy," he said to me in the washroom of the waiters' bunkhouse the night of her arrival at the Center. Cocking his head at an angle, he studied his Byronesque reflection in the wall-to-wall mirror above the washstand, and then grabbed up a couple of bronze-backed hair brushes monogrammed "G.E.M," because wouldn't you know his middle name would be Edmund, the unregenerate, irredeemable creep, and began a fastidious slicking back of that shoulder-length, curly blond hair of his and so help me I was thinking of taking a scythe to it. "Just a little research for my novel," he added, leering and winking at me in the mirror. This did not please me. At all. You keep hearing people say that they enjoy competi-tion. Well, I'm not one of them. I actually fear and *detest* competition, and while I don't have a face that looks like Camembert cheese rinds, this Malloy was much more than good-looking—he was smooth, and like Leo Durocher, the old Brooklyn Dodgers baseball manager that people called Leo "The Lip," he had mastered the knack of dramatizing himself, so that when it came to women, he'd just pose against the back-drop of his graduate studies in journalism at Columbia University, always walking around looking deeply thoughtful and letting it be known that he was working on "a very important novel," a pipe-puffing, aura-of-mystery sort of gambit that made him the Lord Jim of the Catskills, his big killer weapon consisting of this penetrating, soulful look that seemed to say to every targeted woman, "I alone understand you completely." If the jerk had a chapter of his novel for every policeman's daughter he'd seduced, his novel would be longer than *War and Peace* and the just discovered sequel.

And so, "Listen, good buddy," I said to him—I'd heard that's how truck drivers talk—"don't you think that your 'research' has carried you a little past the limits of art and into the dominion of Guiness Book of Records? I speak specifically of Kinsey and his picturesque graphics and reports." After spreading a little talcum powder over his disgustingly handsome face, Malloy grinned at me through the looking glass and, not being calm and unruffleable as Alice, when "Byron Man" taunted, "Jealous, Lofler?", my right hand reflexively balled into a fist to administer "Death without the Sacraments," but my hand was stayed by the music. It was the Center dance combo, a group of high school seniors from Waterbury, Connecticut, who called themselves "The Plainclothesmen," and even though they sounded like galaxies in collision, it meant a chance for the waiters and busboys to mingle with the guests (I was thinking of Miss Harnedy) on the dance floor of the Center's "Huddle Room." One anxious, seething stare into the mirror convinced me that Malloy, too, was thinking of Miss Harnedy but more like a walrus thinking of flounder, so I assembled my shaving gear over a wash stand and moved quicker than that cartoon hero, "The Flash," but almost half an hour later when I got to the Huddle Room I found Terry Harnedy dancing with Malloy. Still, they hadn't gotten cozy as yet because as usual "The Plainclothesmen" were playing an Irish waltz, what most New York cops being Irish or Italian with *Arriverderci Roma* pretty sure to be next, so I sliced through the whirl of bodies on the dance floor like a hoy Damascus blade through Unguentine.

"Cut!" I said, tapping Malloy's shoulder smartly, and possibly a little more smartly than needed, and "Of course!" he had to say, which is the downside of the polished college aesthete, Ashley Wilkes gallantry gambit.

I had counted on this. I am cunning.

So "Hello!" I said, smiling, and "Hello!" she said back, and then brown-eyes and I twirled around at arm's-length, an altogether unsatisfactory arrangement, but then, in their typically unpredictable way, "The Plainclothesmen" eased into *Night and Day*, and, overweeningly impetuous rascal that I am, I tried leaning my head against Terry Harnedy's, this sometimes being the prelude to intimate discussion, but at the touch Terry instantly pulled away her head and stared over my shoulder just like she was looking at Betelgeuse III, either that or the inside of an empty candy bag. I thought of her warmth at breakfast, the interested glances over the kidney pie at lunch, the smile that verged on adoration when at dinner I sneaked her a second caramel-custard.

And yet suddenly she was cooler than yesterday's pancakes.

"Will you be going to Mexico again do you think?" she asked in a distant, disinterested voice.

"Going *where*?" I said.

"To Mexico," she repeated, a concept as likely as Mohandas K. Gandhi and Sitting Bull duetting on "I'm an Indian Too."

"Is this a joke?" I said, laughing a little; "If I go anywhere soon it's back to Georgetown and my boys."

She stopped dancing, her eyes widening as she pull back to stare at me. "*Boys*? You mean you're *married*?" she exclaimed.

"Oh, no no," I said quickly; "The 'boys' are kids from poor families at the Georgetown Boys Club back in D.C. I coach their basketball team and do some tutoring."

"You live in Washington?" she asked with what looked like a frown of perplexity, and, "Partly," I answered; "I'm a junior at Georgetown."

"And Washington's your home?"

I said, "Brooklyn."

She stared blankly for a second, and then tilting back her head she started laughing in a richly husky, throaty way laced with Tinker Bell fairy dust, and then she closed with me again and just danced, still erupting in a giggle or two now and then—oh, sweetest, mysterious fandango of life!—her cheek was now warmly tight against mine, so as you doubtless understand, I didn't try pushing for explanations. Mexico, Schmecksico: I felt happily muddled and childlike again.

"May I cut in, please?"

Loathe to pull my head away from Terry's, I swiveled an eye sideways and felt sick to my stomach at the sight of Malloy's perfect fiz, and on an unthinking impulse I threw aside couth and all it meant to Cole Porter as I growled, "You may have the next waltz, Your Grace, but for now I suggest you get mercifully lost!" so that, trapped in his posture of courtliness with maybe a slight touch of heartburn in the mix, Malloy had to smile and tilt his head forward in a mini-bow and then turn with chin up and back striaght and ooze away. I am a master of psychology.

Or not. Terry pulled her head away, her face pinking up.

"That wasn't very nice," she said a wee bit coolly.

"This is true," I intoned in the same way I would have said, "Guilty with an explanation," and then added, "I just don't like that guy."

"I don't see why," Terry said. She leaned her cheek against mine again, and then after a spurty little giggle, she amended, "On second thought, maybe I do."

"You do?"

I felt her cheek getting warmer.

"Oh, honestly, I don't know how I could have been so stupid!" she began; "Your, ah,—friend, is it?—Gregg Malloy—" Here she started to gaspingly chortle as she recounted, "Well, he was telling me he's writing a novel and—"

"You mean the one that no one's ever seen a word of and when you ask what it's about, Malloy tilts up his chin and he shoots you this mystical stare and says, 'Discussing it would fatally dissipate its energies?' I'm so sorry. You were saying?"

She went, "Hmmm," and, "Well, I asked him some things about *you* and—"

"You asked about *me*?"

"Yes, you, and he said you were a migrant worker."

"*What*?"

"And that summers you worked here as a waiter"—another giggle that continued in spurts through the rest of her statement—"but for the rest of the year you were employed at a tuna cannery in Mexico!"

I said, "I see" as now a sudden intuition gripped my shoulders and shook me that although she seemed warm and down to earth and not a snob of any shape or dimension, still and all, being the police commissioner's daughter, Terry Harnedy's men had to have a certain dignity about them, which was bad, as this made her particularly susceptible to suave phony novelist types like Gregg Malloy, who was staring blue death rays at me from the sidelines, may his eyes become Medusa's and roll up and stare inward.

"Say, my Dad's coming up here at the end of the week," Terry told me as she snuggled in pleasingly close, "and I'd really, really like you to meet him." The second "really" was significant. I slept well.

⸺

And woke up to a nightmare when at eight the next morning the thirty-eight guests at my tables came pouring through the dining room doors like famished trout into a government stocked pond. No other waiter's guests, mark you. No. Only mine. Most guests usually dribbled in for breakfast anywhere from half past eight until ten and now here they were and all at once!

Well, I tried. First I went to the Moser's table where they wanted two oatmeals, one Post Toasties, one Wheaties, and two Shredded Wheats, one with whole milk and the other with skim.

"And what for eggs today?" asked Mrs. Moser.

"Only scrambled and boiled, ma'am."

"Really? No basted?"

"I'm sorry."

"Oh, well, then, Mr. Moser and I will have three-minute eggs. And you, Andy?" she asked the two-year-old in the high chair.

"I don't *want* none!" he bawled.

"Three-minute eggs for him also," said his mother; "The older children will have two-minute eggs and for little Chester, a 90-second job, and he'll have it *before* his cereal."

"Is he one of the oatmeals?"

"No, the Wheaties."

Are you grasping this? We didn't write the orders down, we remembered them!

I saw them glaring at me from over at the Carey table so I went there right away for their orders. "Mornin, Officer Carey!" I greeted with totally phony relish.

"Mornin' Lofler! Look, just coffee for me to start. And would you bring it right away? I can't see straight 'til I've had my first cup."

Just then someone at the Kurtz table hollered out for me and seconds later *all* my guests had gotten into the mood and started joining the increasingly testy chorus while two little boys who were red-haired and freckled and no doubt alumni of the old *Hoody Doody Show* on TV started banging their forks and spoons against glasses and plates, at which, smiling reassuringly, I raised an arm and waved my hand all around at my tables as if to say I had everything under control, which was doubtless what Custer did with his troops about a minute before the start of the Battle of Little Big Horn, and then quick-like I turned and made tracks toward the swinging doors that led into the kitchen, but as I made to enter I ran into the blistering gaze of "Wild Willie" Dolan, the Center's headwaiter, who was just coming out. Red-eyed and bald, except for two elfish tufts of white hair behind his ears and a few scattered single strands atop his head, Dolan folded his arms and gritted hoarsely and pretty much loud enough for everyone to hear, "What in blue thunder's going on here?" and "I don't know," I told Dolan, answering softly like the good book says, but if it "turned away wrath" I was unable to detect it inasmuch as Dolan now raised his voice even louder. "If you find it *impossible* to handle your tables," he threatened, "we can *always* divert you to the dishwashing unit!" I heard laughter and I sneaked a look around and everyone was staring at us, bemused, and with their eyebrows lifted up. All except one person. Terry. She was staring through a floor to ceiling window at Indian Head Mountain in the near distance with a sort of funny look on her face and I speak not at all of funny "*ha ha*."

◆

Unkempt, unhaloed and unstrung, I shambled into my room right after the dinner serving and flopped face-down on my cot. Was I feeling despondent, you ask? Does Charlie Chan like egg foo yung?

From his bunk across from mine, Charlie Price, a seventeen-year-old busboy and my bunkmate, was appraising me from underneath droopy lids. Tall and lanky and about to be a high school senior, he had lusterless, whale-gray, beady eyes and a W. C. Fieldish bulbous, red-tipped nose.

"So 'Wild Willie' lowered the boom on you," I heard the kid twanging in his colorless and adenoidal voice.

"Yup," I answered dismally into my pillow.

"And all your guests came in for breakfast at the same time this morning?"

"I am running out of yups."

"And of course you have no interest in hearing how come?"

I turned over, sat up, then swung my legs over the side of the cot, and, clasping my hands together I hunched over, head down, and with the whites of my eyes very strongly in evidence as I lifted a glowering stare up to Charlie, assuring him, "The level of my interest is deep!"

Charlie reached into a front flap pocket of his khaki "For God and Empire" shorts, slipped out a slightly creased two-by-four inch card that he handed across to me with a quietly portentous, "*Read this!*"

I took it and read it. It was one of the Center's official announcement cards, with "Police Recreation Center" engraved in black lettering at the top, while below it was the following typed advisory: "Please take notice that breakfast will be served tomorrow morning, Monday, between 8 and 8:30 only so that needed repairs may be made in the kitchen and prior to the day's luncheon service."

It was signed, "William Dolan, Director."

I looked up at Charlie. "But only *my* guests came in at eight!"

"Forsooth." This was one of Charlie's two favorite expressions, the second one being completely unknown to me, Charlie having explained to me that it was "secret" and "I only like to say it to myself."

"Maybe only *your* guests got the cards," Charlie uttered with portent.

"What do you mean?"

"I mean maybe I also saw a certain longhaired waiter slipping them under only certain guests' doors last night."

I looked off and muttered dazedly, "I've been juiced!"

"Indeed. And I have even *more* exhilarating news."

I shifted wary eyes to him. "Such as what?"

"Like where Terry's going to be at half past eight, which is down at the spaghetti place with this waiter whose eye you are wishing the Grim Reaper would catch."

"The spaghetti place?" I gaped at him in horror.

"The spaghetti place."

Leaning over, I lowered my head into both my hands and quietly murmured, "Disaster."

The "spaghetti place" was a tiny woodframe home not far from the driveway leading up to the Center. It was owned by a little old Italian couple who during summer nights turned their dining room into a make-shift Italian restaurant for workers at the Center who wanted a break from a diet of Irish stew with "sautéed shamrock drizzle." Serving only spaghetti with red sauce, rolls and the cheapest available chianti, the old couple had so tiny a margin of profit that instead of plastic grapes hanging down in the dining room, there were *photos* of plastic grapes. The clear and present danger about the spaghetti place was the romantic walk back on that hibiscus smelling, apple tree-lined road, most especially if there happened to be moonlight, plus you heard the nearby splashing of little Bridal Veil Falls as well as songbirds outdoing themselves thinking one night St. Francis of Assisi might come by and even the crickets being discreet deliberately lowering the volume on their chirping. The walk was Creep Malloy's favorite and, by all accounts, a sure-fire prelude to Close Encounters of the Most Desired Kind, and tonight, as it happened, the moon was to be full!

I grieved, "Charlie, I *like* this girl!"

"Good for you. So when it's dark why don't you moose down the hill to the spaghetti place, wait outside, and when Terry and Malloy come out you just say to him, "Cut!" then take Terry by hand and say you're walking her back."

"Oh, come on!"

"No, it will work, Master," Charlie intoned with an accent meant to imitate the giant genie in the movie *The Thief of Bagdad*; "Everyone is knowing this Malloy, he be—"

"Charlie, quit it. I'm just not in the mood."

"Understood. Look, what I'm saying is Malloy is chicken and will fold like a fan in the hand of a ticked off Geisha."

"And if he doesn't?"

"Then you bust him in the chops."

"This is not the way of Zen," I said; "Bad. A very bad idea."

"I give you goodies and you answer me with Oriental farts."

"Farts are morally neutral," I primly riposted.

I could almost hear Charlie's big bushy eyebrows sickling up as he said to me, "*Why*, Pete? *Why* is it bad?"

"It isn't dignified, Charlie."

"It isn't *what*?!"

Here I lifted my head and eyed him.

I said, "Chazz, I have read the runes and for numerous reasons that are far too innumerable to enumerate, they are telling me Miss Harnedy feels about dignity in men the way Frank Lloyd Wright must have felt about Euclid," I fnished, omitting mention of how St. Simeon Stylites felt about him, and with this I looked back down at my shoes and my woes.

"Me, I wonder how dignified Malloy would look stretched out on the road on his kisser," I heard Charlie ruminating darkly; "It wouldn't come to that, though," he went on; "Malloy's even scared of Willie Dolan's chihuahua. Hey, Pete, do you remember—"

And abruptly I heard only the sound of silence, and then bedsprings creaking sharply and then running shoes thumping to the floor, and looking up I saw that Charlie was now sitting on the edge of his cot with his normally narrow slits for eyes that gave him the look of a drowsy cobra now wide and lit up like *aurora borealis*, as "*Pete!*", he declared with excitement, "You remember the night we walked home from the movies and you scared the living urine out of? You remember?"

Not only did I remember, but, being possessed of oracular powers that, had word of them ever reached her, would have sent the storied Sybil at Cumae into deep depression and to reading books like *I'm Okay, You're Okay*, and almost anything else about self-esteem, I had an instant intuition of what Charlie had in mind, and "Knock it off!" I very quickly and testily rumbled; "You're a kid and that is definitely kid stuff out the kazoo!"

"But it'll work, Pete! Don't you see? You've got this gift!"

"I said, forget it! It's too childish for words!"

Around a quarter to nine I was on my way down to the "spaghetti place" with Charlie, locked and loaded and ready to carry out his plan: for the love of Terry Harnedy I was ready to revert to infancy, and even mutter "Rosebud" any number of times. With the moon obscured by clouds, the darkness was inky black so that Charlie stumbled up against me when the road took a sharp and sudden turn to the left, and there, up ahead and close by, we saw the brightly glowing entry lanterns on each side of the "Spaghetti House's" front door, which right away came open as a man and a woman and two little kids came out, and "Come on!" I whispered huskily at Charlie as I tugged him by his blue and white Brooklyn Prep sweatshirt toward a clump of tall four-foot-high grass where we hid ourselves, and waited for whoever it was to pass by, which was fairly soon when the door to the spaghetti house opened and a group came out, a man and a woman and two kids. We instantly ducked down our heads, and when the people passed I thought I recognized the voice of the man as a cop named Kurtz, who was a guest at my tables, though I couldn't be absolutely sure inasmuch as when they passed us I was busy plucking thistles off the collar of my T-shirt that were stinging my neck. Then the family's voices faded and we stood up and bided our time as we awaited the Main Event and now with butterflies beginning to flutter around in my stomach.

"And so how did you come by your gift?" Charlie asked me with this earnest and concerned kind of social worker interest in his voice like I was Jeanne Val Jean at the age of nineteen and he was building my case file so he could authorize trading in the silver that I'd stolen from a Catholic church for food stamps. "You've never really told me," he finished.

"Yes, I did but you've forgotten," I answered him curtly, a little edgy and testy about what was coming up, "or is this going to be the sequel to *Of Mice and Men* where you keep asking me to tell you again about the rabbits?"

Charlie quietly said, "No."

I said, "Okay, then, for the second time: I first did it after seeing Lon Chaney in the movie *The Wolfman*. Are you happy?"

"It's just so freakily convincing," Charlie uttered with a note of appre-hensiveness in his voice wedged in there along with all the slobbering awe, and at the same time he was searching my face intently as if for signs of hairs sprouting from my ears and from my nose, and then we suddenly crouched lower down into the grass as a door-shaped slab of light was scooped out of the dimness and through it came the heartbeat I was constantly listening for, and behind her that creep, that fraud, that were some horrible misfortune to suddenly strike him, I would feel more *schadenfreude* than all of Germany, Austria, and Lower Saxony could ever hope to contain. The door closed and I couldn't see the hoax-crossed couple any more so I waited for their sauntering footsteps to approach and move past us, along with their warm and semi-intimate laughter and quiet chatter that was making me totally nuts, and when they'd passed clenched my jaw and was totally ready to do this "Thing" that I had to do and that I'd done at the Center only once before out of madcap exuberance and for Charlie's edification right after we'd seen *Frankenstein Meets the Wolfman* at the movie house in nearby Tannersville Village; yes, the very "Thing," as someone afterwards recounted, that once caused Baskerville, the Center director's giant hound, to hunker down whimpering and trembling with fear, or at the least, most observers agreed, deep unease. Charlie's theory was it might cause a similar and—shall we say, "undignified?"—response in a certain waiter-novelist whose name wasn't Dostoievski and which I was hoping to turn to mud. So now I gulped down a lungful of cool night air mixed with equal parts brazenness, desperation, and The Red Queen's maddest, most impetuous whim, cupped my hands to my mouth, raised my head, and cut loose with a blood-chilling, ululating howl you would swear it was Lon Chaney's movie werewolf cry! The sound of gasps and running feet blended nicely with the end of it, a forlorn and descending, weakening whine that died in my throat with a sorrowful whimper as if the werewolf was having regrets, and as I lowered my hands the full moon had momentarily slipped out from behind the clouds revealing Charlie standing petrified, his eyes wide and shiny and staring and his arms held stiffly at his sides like some acned, teenaged Bronxville zombie, a sight that was mercifully covered over when clouds obscured the moon again and there was darkness, "Chazz, snap out of it!" I ordered him huskily. He came to and shook his head, and seemed about to make some comment but I shushed him as from somewhere up the road I heard rave reviews, though unfortunately not from Gregg Molloy. It was the Kurtz kids, whimpering and sobbing, and their mother trying to calm them down.

I turned a questioning, rueful look to Charlie.

"Collateral damage," he said with a shrug.

I said, "No. 'Friendly fire.'"

"War is war."

Settled back comfortably on reclining chairs on the Center's second floor patio and looking as loose as two giant boiled noodles, Charlie and I had to struggle not to grin and show the world we were eating our cookies as Malloy, slightly limping, and with Terry beside him, came breathlessly stumbling up the winding stone steps from below and flopped down into chairs facing ours. Charlie and I had raced back to the Center through a shortcut in the woods that I knew, where, at Charlie's insistence that we needed "insurance," I'd paused to cut loose another call of the wild, before taking our positions barely a minute before.

"Oh, man!" Malloy wheezed, still catching his breath.

"Hey, what happened? Sprain your ankle?" Charlie asked him.

"So flipping dark out there!" He reached a hand to the injured ankle, checking it tenderly for soreness and swelling, I suppose, as he added, "Yeah, I fell. I fell running."

"You were running? What for?" Charlie asked.

Malloy lifted his head in mild disbelief. "'What *for*'? Didn't you hear that wolf howling out there? It was loud enough to wake up the dead!"

Charlie looked incredulous, his forte.

"In the Catskills? Are you serious?" he snorted; "A *wolf*?"

"Oh, well, I heard it, too. It *was* a wolf. I grew up on a ranch in Montana and I know that sound quite well."

We all turned to the source of the somehow chirpy yet cracked leather voice. It was a little old lady who was seated with a bigger old lady about eight or ten feet away. "Blood-curdling, it was. I heard it twice."

"Oh, me too!" chimed in the bigger old lady, "and it sounded like a wolf to me as well, a very angry and troubled one."

I decided it was time for judicious intervention.

I said, "Maybe someone's *imitating* a wolf."

Twisting around in her chair and fixing me gravely with a glittering eye, "Young man," the little old lady intoned, "I assure you nothing human could have made that sound."

"Yes, that's exactly how we felt about it, too," Gregg Malloy was quick to agree. I mean, Miss Harnedy here and I." He turned to Terry, whose expression, while placid, was somehow strange, as he said, "It was terrifying, Terry, right?" and turning back to the elderly women, Malloy told them, "We ran back here as fast as we could!" And then, dear reader, dear patient, understanding heart, my cup, as they say, ranneth over as Terry turned an expressionless stare to Malloy saying, "Gregg, I didn't think it was scary at all. The only reason I ran was to try to catch up to you."

Malloy's face turned the color of a psychedelic lark in a Van Gogh wheatfield. "I could use a cold drink," he said quietly to no one as he lifted his arm and started winding his Christina Rossetti wristwatch as he asked, "What do you say we check the soda fountain, Terry? They're still open, I think."

"You go ahead, Gregg, I'll join you in a minute," she told him.

Suspicious, reluctant, and apprehensive, Malloy looked me in the eye and, standing, held my gaze as he answered, "Sure. Should I order for you?"

"A lemon Coke, please."

"Okay."

Malloy turned and, chin up and shoulders back, he walked stiffly and slowly toward the hotel lobby entry doors as if about to receive some high award, either that or a beating by Turkish prison guards, and then Charlie,

too, stood up with an obviously feigned big stretch and yawn and a muttered, "Oh, well, bedtime for Bonzo, you guys," as with this he turned and,
erratically lurching from side, beetled away toward the staircase that would
lead him to the grounds and the waiters' and busboys' bunkhouse. "Goodnight, Charlie!" Terry called after him, at which Charlie raised a languid
hand into the air as, not turning, he answered, "Yeah, yeah."

Terry turned to appraise me the way Frankenstein must have first
looked at his monster, which was doubtless with mixed emotions, especially if when it opened its eyes it looked unhappy.

"Haven't seen very much of you today," I said blithely, imitating how
I thought Cary Grant would have said it, but Terry wasn't buying as her
eyes seemed to narrow with suspicion as she asked me, "Where were you
when that animal cried out?" to which, parrying as skillfully as Scara-
mouche while his hand is groping frantically behind his back for the wall
brick that when pressed will open up the secret door to escape, I put on my
Max Beerbohm's "Lord George Hell" saintly mask and said innocently,
"Why?"

"Why?" Terry leaned her face close in to mine with a look of mock
wonder and a sly and sardonic smile as, "Why, Grandma," she lilted in a
Little Red Riding Hood piping, young voice, "what great big eyes you
have!" Then she reached a hand down to a cuff of my trousers, and, plucking something off it, straightened up and pressed it into my hand, which
I can tell you really smarted because it was a thistle.

"I'll keep your demented secret, little boy," Terry told me with an edge
of cool contempt in her voice, and with that she stood and headed for the
lobby entrance.

I jumped up and called out to her, "Terry!" and she stopped and turned
her head to me so quickly that for an unexpected moment of accidental
grace a framing tress of her long, wavy, chestnut hair fell against her cheek.
"Yes?" she said, and in her voice I heard a softly rising note of expectation,
or maybe it was hope, or maybe both, but being taken aback, almost
stunned, by the moment's revelation, not merely of Terry's physical beauty,

but of something mysterious and almost otherworldly about her, like a momentary flash of something like remembrance, or even beyond that, recognition, and now there she was before me, standing and waiting for my answer, but in my brain-locked, dream-locked, cow-kicked-by-a-monkey daze, the only words to slip out from my lips were an almost unconscious, numbly murmured, "Never mind," and in the instant Terry's eyes lost their light and whatever had caused that light to shine and she turned a crisp heel, striding quickly and entering the hotel lobby, where through the glass façade I saw her heading for the soda fountain and Malloy and very soon she had vanished from my blundering sight.

The next day after breakfast service, I was resting on a patio recliner in a state of geometrically expanding funk. My attempt about an hour before to reignite the *status quo antewolfum* through a humorous appeal to sloppy sentimentality by pouring a little coffee on Terry's dry cereal while at the same time attempting to evoke *Casablanca* rasping in Humphrey Bogart's sandpaper voice, "We'll always have the Bran Flakes and coffee," which garnered me nothing but an incredulous glare. Bad enough. But now who comes up to me hefting a .22 caliber rifle along with maybe five other cops in a tight little semi-circle behind him who are likewise toting extended heat, but patrolman Herbie "Depth Bomb" Kurtz, whose kids I might have terrorized the night before. "You know how to use one of these?" Kurtz asked me, holding up the rifle lest his meaning evade my grasp, and when I nodded and told him that I did, he turned and nodded in vindication at his comrades, saying quietly, "See? I can always tell." He then turned back to me and asked if I'd be willing to join "a sort of *ad hoc* posse," I believe is how he put it, formed to hunt down and kill "the freaking goddam wolf" that was "scaring the living shit out of people," citing mothers and wives and little children in particular. I felt a tingling up the back of my neck. Was this real or some kind of "sting" operation?

"Mr. Dolan says you've been here lots of summers before," Kurtz droned on in a monotone like Jack Webb as Sergeant Friday on *Dragnet*, and with a dead shark expression in his close-set eyes, "and are exceedingly prone to have knowledge of the area and are therefore a valuable posse asset. So whaddya say," he concluded, "are you with us?"

I said, "Sure, but are we doing this now, right this minute?"

"Yes, now," Kurtz answered me grimly, the twin rotted rosary beads he had for eyes drilling into mine as he went with a seething intensity, "And after lunch and after dinner every day and every night until we nail this fucking noisy wolf bastard!"

I said, "I'll have to be back in time to set up for lunch."

"*Si, hombre*," grunted Kurtz, whose precinct was in "Little Puerto Rico" in the Bronx.

"You know, I think my roommate Charlie would be a really good man to have along," I suggested, and then mentioning that Charlie went to Xavier. "It's a Jesuit military high school," I said to them.

They gave me another rifle for Charlie.

I found him down at the horseshoe pits tossing lazily floating one-and-three-quarters, and after explaining about the posse and all I had to slap him around a little bit on account of he was laughing like a rummed up kookabura and I couldn't seem to get him to stop. Also, Sergeant Kurtz was waiting. Charlie sobered up in time for us to join the so-called "Search Committee," with all these cops looking somber and frowning just like we were about to nail Dillinger, and I worked it so Charlie and I were paired up, and together off we went, heads high, guns loaded and faces barely straight, and it only took to maybe about eleven-thirty as we were boringly feigning searching for the wolf in a field of chest high wild grass not too far from that Center's main building that Charlie dragged us headlong into madness and peril by suggesting that—how did he put it?—"in all fairness," I could give the other hunters a "much keener sense of mission" if I were to cut loose with a werewolf howl!

"You mean *now*?"

"Yes, now."

"Are you *crazy*?"

Joey held up an index fnger. "Only one."

"They might *shoot* us!" I squalled.

"Pete, none of these guys could hit the broad side of a barn with a banjo! They're all traffic cops!"

"But *why*, Charlie? Why take the chance?"

Charlie shrugged and said laconically, "Why not?"

Well, we traded level stares for about six seconds, and maybe we'd been tramping around bareheaded under August sunlight for a bit too long, but then I grinned and dropped my rifle as on a sudden and uncontrollable impulse, I raised my head, cupped my hands around my mouth, gulped in a lungful of mischievous air and cut loose with a werewolf cry that would have made even Bela Lugosi blanch, and when I'd finished and looked down with a smile at Charlie, he was giving me that same creepy mesmerized stare pretty much the same way that he'd done the night before. I said "Charlie, relax! It's just me!"

Except it wasn't. Charlie was goggling at "Wild Willie" Dolan!

———————

Like Dante's vision of Hell, the Center's kitchen's dishwashing unit contained levels of wretched degredation and these were known as "Scraper," "Stacker," and "Sorter." The Scraper used a rubber squeegee to push food scraps off the plates that the busboys brought in, while the Stacker arrange the squeegeed plates in wooden racks that were pushed into a steam driven cleansing device called "The Box," and when they came out in a burning-hot state, it was the Sorter's job to pluck them back out of the racks and then to sort them and stack them on a broad metal apron forming an entire side of the unit where the waiters would pick up clean dishes for their pre-meal set-ups. Have we got that? Good. You can't *believe* how good. So by the morning of the second day following the werewolf hunt, and at the end of breakfast service, the cast and crew of the morality play that was to come were in place. Charlie was the Scraper and I was the Sorter, while a teenaged local kid, Jim Clark, was kept in place as Stacker.

"So what's new on the Harnedy front?" Charlie asked me as he squeegeed pasty lima bean fragments from a plate with neither shame nor contrition for our present lowly state, and "Oh, why hell, she just adores me since I got this new job," I nearly snarled as I jerked a rack of dishes from The Box; "My God, the girl can't keep her hands off me, Charlie."

"Why don't you tell her you're doing research for a novel about dishwashers?"

I was about to make a churlish retort when fairest Fate made its "entrance with its usual flair" as the swinging doors between the kitchen and the dining room suddenly pushed open and into the kitchen came trooping not only Willie Dolan, flushed and beaming with pride, but also Terry Harnedy and her father, the New York Police Commissioner himself!

"The kitchen layout," "Wild Willie" was burbling, his arm up and waving around surrealistically; "It's all arranged for maximum serving speed. And the dishwashing unit"—he turned and I took a step back toward The Box as he pinned me with a withering glance—"the dishwashing unit," he repeated, "is a mechanized and highly efficient assembly-line operation!"

The Commissioner, a gray-haired, kindly looking elf of a guy, just sort of nodded and as Dolan went on with his spiel I thought I ought to look busy, so I picked up a stack of saucers, carried them over to the apron, set them down, and at last had the guts to lift my head and look at Terry, a bit of wasted derring-do, it turned out, since she studiously avoided looking back. Standing stiffly, both her hands in the pockets of a green silk jacket, her attention seeming fixed upon "Wild Willie," in her face and in her posture I was reading confusion and uncertainty, even a struggle to keep looking away. Ah, but then came the good and the true part, the part about Fate, which doesn't always necessarily have to be crummy, for now in through the swinging doors breezed Malloy, looking jaunty and slicker than snot, and sizing up the situation in a sweeping and condescending glance, he swooped over to the apron, pounding on it hard with the flat of a hand you would have thought was meant exclusively for playing the klavichord, and with an air of authority and easy command he said, "Step it up, Lofler! I need salad plates! Forty! In a hurry! Get cracking!"

Looking past him, I saw that Terry all of a sudden was watching as was everyone else in the kitchen, and, "Oh, good! A chance to see our team in action now, Commissioner! Beautiful!" brayed "Wild Willie" as Jim Clark had already pushed a rack of salad plates through "The Box," and as soon as they were out I made a show out of casually plucking them out of the rack, and after stacking up a pile of twenty of them, I picked up the darlings with both my hands and, ever eager to serve and please, slowly ambled to the "apron" humming *My Way.* Are you with me? Ahead of me? Perhaps. You see, the first time you pick up a dish that's just come out of "The "Box," what you do is you wince, you yelp, and you drop it, there even being scattered reports of vivid cursing and spewing of profanities. But then after you've worked a day or two as a Sorter, the dishes will only feel lukewarm, even though to all others they will still feel hotter than a pizza oven in Cairo, most especially to a waiter with sensitive hands. Did that thought cross my mind as I casually set down the stack of salad plates on the apron in front of Malloy? Does Dracula have fangs? Oh, moy dears, what a glorious, fantabulous, miraculous sight blessed my eyes as I watched Malloy pick up the stack and then drop them, yelping "YOW!," and then "Holy *Freak*!" as every lettuce-loving, tomato-hugging sweetheart of a salad plate slipped from his hands and went crashing and smashing to the floor!

Terry's father looked slightly bemused, while two hairs on Willie Dolan's bald head stood up in shock screaming, "What in thunderation was *that*?!" a non-event since no one listens to inanimate objects. I of course turned a gauging look to Terry, and after a moment or two of uncertainty, she turned and caught my eye and I winked. For a second she looked startled, then a hand flew to her mouth to cover over a spouting giggle of realization and—so help me!—when she turned and saw Gregg Malloy's petrified expression she put a hand to her cheek and burst into that Mercedes Cambridge Tinker Bell laughter! Lads, I thought she'd never stop! And you know what? Now and then when I pick up a towel to help her dry the dishes, the missus gets this impish, twinkly smile in her eyes and starts laughing all over again, just remembering. Once she even leaned her lovely head on my shoulder, saying fondly as she wore a slight smile, "Pete, I would have loved you even if you'd been the Scraper."

But of course, that never was the case as Gregg Malloy turned out to be the Center's speediest, most talented Scraper ever and I wouldn't have deprived him of his squeegee for the world. Nevertheless, as I am known in some quarters as "Firm But Fair Lofler" and ever ready to forgive once I've had my revenge, I'll admit that in one respect I had judged Gregg Malloy quite rashly, for as it turns out he really *was* working on a novel, which I know because it's going to be published this September. I've also had a chance to skim through a copy of the uncorrected bound galleys which came into my hands because of my work, which as it happens is for the *New York Times Sunday Book Review.* Of course, I'm recusing myself from this one, but I suspect Malloy's novel is in for a bit of a bumpy ride. The opening line of his Chapter One is, "Last night, I dreamt I went to Manderly again."

THE END

INDEX